YOUNG FARMER SEEKS WIFE

The Arts Council
An Chomhairle Ealaíon

The Publishers gratefully acknowledge the financial assistance
of The Arts Council/An Chomhairle Ealaíon

First published in 2002 by Marino Books
An imprint of Mercier Press
16 Hume Street Dublin 2
Tel: (01) 661 5299; Fax: (01) 661 8583
E-mail: books@marino.ie
Website: www.mercier.ie

Trade enquiries to CMD Distribution
55A Spruce Avenue
Stillorgan Industrial Park
Blackrock County Dublin
Tel: (01) 294 2560; Fax: (01) 294 2564
E-mail: cmd@columba.ie

© Nicholas Furlong 2002

ISBN 1 86023 147 0
10 9 8 7 6 5 4 3

A CIP record for this title is available
from the British Library

Cover design by Liam Furlong at
Space D&C

Printed in Ireland by ColourBooks,
Baldoyle Industrial Estate, Dublin 13

Young Farmer Seeks Wife

Nicholas Furlong

At the instigation of Mairéad Breslin
and Donagh MacDonagh

CONTENTS

1

The Lost Lamb

This account which I have determined to write will be unique. I have read a lot of books. Some of them were very good and some of them were dirty. One common denominator was possessed by the lot of them: the victory of the lead character over many obstacles. Most of them concerned his triumphs with women of high and low degree and, if he didn't marry them in the end, he had the satisfaction of committing a serious sin of impurity several times with no ill effects. That's a far cry from what the missioner said – namely, that the adulterer went out of his mind.

I refer to works I have studied. One, by a Mr Miller, introduces us to enterprises of an immoral nature, none of which ends in defeat. Then I read of the facility of Mr Stephen Vizinczey since the age of twelve with women of middle years. John Philip Lundin was highly successful with every woman he laid his hands on; it didn't matter whether it was in Tokyo, Seoul, Florence or Paris. He emerged from the last page without a scratch on him and no trace of disease or insanity.

I have given this matter great thought and I think it is high time that an account of the many reverses that really happen was given. I will tell of what it's like to be made a hunt of and let down and refused, and if I'm not greatly mistaken, I'll be the first to do so in the history of the world.

I'd better explain a bit of background. I was born of most respectable parents in Mulgannon, Wexford, on 2 March 1929. My father died young, of Phibb's disease. My eldest sister also died young and I'm all that's left, bar the mother. The mother always thought very highly of me. We were never hungry, nor, I am informed, were my mother's people or my father's people.

We have six neighbours in this townland but I have a lot of enemies. One of them is a raw Kerrywoman who used to teach. She lives down the road from us with children in the civil service and on the missions. She made out when I was a child that I must have been swapped in the pram by the fairies. Her name is Nellie MacDonagh. The only thing in her favour is her youngest son who is not a bit like her or anyone else in the house. I heard the mother say that he is after a tangler. He is a right sort and has plenty of brains without the appearance of it. I knew by his oul' wan that she reckoned I had led her boy to sin. MacDonagh's father was a prefect in the Holy Family Confraternity and the Vincent de Paul. Mr MacDonagh was a marshal with a big yellow sash and collar at the annual Corpus Christi procession and it was well known that the Holy Name never left his lips except in prayer.

Now that I've mentioned MacDonagh I might as well mention Mulcahy. Mulcahy was what is known in Wexford as an afterclap. This Barony of Forth dialect word indicates that, many years after his previous brother was born, Mulcahy was born. His father and mother, Mr and Mrs Mulcahy of Mulgannon House, sent him away to college and he used to come home decorated with a college scarf. Mulcahy junior was very big, six feet tall and broad in proportion. He suffered from the knowledge that it was a mortal sin to keep company unless you intended to marry, and also that to touch, see or think about the private part of the person for the sake of pleasure was a deliberate mortal sin. If you did give in to yourself and went to sleep that night unrepentant, and gas filled the room and you died, you would be in hell forever, roaring, with your eyeballs falling out on your jaws by dint of the furnace flames' sear. That concept would be bad enough, but Mulcahy was tempted by the vice of impurity if he only saw a crow swinging on a gate.

This problem, coupled with the fact that he occasionally gave in to himself, made him a bit odd. Mulcahy had humours according to the phase of the moon. He'd go off into long spasms of brooding and loss of spirits – take the face off you if you were to pass a remark. He didn't smoke or drink and he was a great footballer and hurler. His father had a big car, which he used to remove under the privacy of darkness. To give him his due, Mulcahy would take us off and talk about life's problems for hours, with special attention to transgressions against the Sixth and Ninth Commandments and the inevitable insanity of habitual transgressors.

The mother told me to avoid the company of girls until I was thirty-five or so and then marry a good sensible match, a respectable girl with a farm and money. 'Take your time, Nicholas,' the mother said. 'There are thousands of farmers' daughters with their tongues hanging out to be married and don't worry about a thing for, after my day, you'll have this place free of rent forever and your uncle Dick's place as well. Who else is he going to leave it to, and him without chick or child? Although he's that crooked, it wouldn't surprise me if he left all to the servant girl. I never liked him. Too sweet. A thwarter.'

That was the mother's notion of my uncle Dick. Richard Furlong, my father's only and unmarried brother, was a great man. If gentle breeding challenged nature to produce a being who in form, mind and elegance of chat would manifest its selective genius, Richard Furlong would have been its proud retort. He was not comprised of one personality but three personalities. And what is more, he had presence. Of a farming background, he was always immaculately dressed, and long after the fashion, he persisted in a hard bowler hat, an indication of his spit upon convention.

He had an immense girth, the size of which was emphasised by narrowing legs and the smallest pair of twinkling feet in patent-leather shoes. A shiny collar, a tie at all times and a suit of dark hue clothed him. The only gesture to flamboyance was the presence upon his watch-chain of medals for step-dancing, old-time waltz, poetry and recitation. Of the last, he received astonished acclaim on his first appearance at Feis Carman in 1914. Youth still claims him and he contrived to enter and win trophies for old-time waltzes. Indeed, his presence was often advertised in announcements of such events. The mother said this was done on purpose to drive him further out of his mind.

His whiskey-red puss could conjure up contempt with greater facility than any other human I know. It could be when I quoted something the mother said, or it could be the mention of an insurance man or agricultural adviser. Both latter groups he denounced as wasters. Whenever I opened my mouth to venture an opinion he turned like vinegar and indicated that I was a three-quarter. Nevertheless, he often pushed a fiver into my hand and said wickedly, 'Here, to hell, put that in your pocket and don't be going around like an ass in a forest.' Five pounds. It was a week's wages. I was never able to summon up thanks, and I knew he didn't want me to say thanks.

And then – the other side of the coin – he destroyed me with more women than I can count. He thought, I suppose, that I hadn't the wit to manage my own business. The first time in my life I ever isolated a girl in company and had a great chance of advancing myself in her favours, who was to make a bags of the issue? Richard Big-Mouth Furlong.

It was a young and happy boy who was left outside in a pony and trap munching biscuits and lemonade while the uncle Dick drank his fill in Mrs Kavanagh's off the Main Street of Screen village. Nicholas Furlong was a maiden boy of fifteen years of age and he had walked thirty head of black polly bullocks there from the fair of Wexford. As I was there in the sun, sucking a bull's-eye, up the road came a grand girl with black hair, brown skin that shone in the sun and eyes dancing in her head. She was on a man's bicycle, pedalling like mad. She caught sight of me and slowed down.

'Eh, boy!' said she. 'Did you see my lamb?'

Prodded into resentment, I didn't bother asking her what lamb; I only said that I'd more to do than to be looking out for her or her lamb.

'My heart is broken looking for the lamb. Where is it?'

I looked in the door of the shop and saw the uncle just laying a green note on the counter. (He always bought for the shop so that he'd be known as gentry or an awful decent sort.)

'I'll find your lamb for you,' I said, and off we trotted, up the lanes above Screen, where the hills are low and the fern-bordered fields have all sorts of strange sea-sand flowers.

She acquired a cruel fondness for me and if I'd pass a remark she'd smile with a flash of dimple. I found out that she was an only girl with one brother, a big farm, a circus of machinery and other property and, though her brother would get the place, she was to get the money.

We couldn't find sight or light of the lamb anywhere. To tell you the truth I didn't care if the lamb was drowned and

11

every lamb in Screen along with it, I was that delighted with her. I asked her if she'd come to *Mutiny on the Bounty* next Saturday night in the Cinema Palace in Wexford town. She said she would. I picked a fistful of blackberries and gave them to her. We talked until it was cold.

When I got back to the pony and trap the uncle was there, prancing up and down the road, cutting briars with his stick and frothing out of the mouth.

'Where were you, the curse of hell light down on you?' he said. I was very taken aback but I said nothing. 'I'll give you something to do with your time,' says he. 'Get aboard to be goddamned and don't slacken reins till we get to Castlebridge.'

He turned on the girl and eyed her up and down from heel to head as if she were a bullock. There was no word passed but she faced him with her hands on her hips and her legs open. A smirk crossed his face.

'Have you no mother, girl, to be out with the likes of this puike, who hasn't the price of a bootlace in his pocket?' (He jingled the money in his own pocket whilst in his oratory.) 'I know what I'd do if you were mine,' he said. 'I'd cover your back with cuts of an ashplant.'

'Faith,' she returned with impudence to Richard Furlong, 'if that's your attitude you can go to *Mutiny on the Bounty* with the fool yourself. He wouldn't see a lamb if it was tied out of him.'

The uncle Dick tipped his hat and heaved himself into the trap. Though no other exchange took place between them, I was certain that some communication of purpose had been dispatched. The last I saw of her was standing in the same brazen stance. As she faded into the distance the uncle Dick rose up and knocked squalls of hair off the pony amid a shower of sparks from the road and bellows of boorish, inane laughter.

'*Mutiny on the Bounty*, be Christ, you goddamn whelp, *Mutiny on the Bounty!*'

This girl later married into a post office, a situation to which there is attached great security. I repaired to my companions and gave them a complete account of what had transpired. MacDonagh formed the opinion that I was no good. He expressed disappointment with my lack of pluck and submitted that had he got the same chance he would have induced her to collaborate in a sin of intimacy. My uncle Richard would not be as big a mug. In fact he proposed that my uncle would exploit the girl to his own pleasure, an experience of which he had practice.

Mulcahy dismissed this by saying that this particular sin, if availed of by my uncle, offended against the civil as well as the religious law. You could get three years up the line and be destroyed. One of my uncle's age does not suffer from either temptation or ability to commit a grievous sin of a carnal nature. At the same time, were such as my uncle to succeed in the biological act, a heart attack was not unknown to occur simultaneously. 'Not,' Mulcahy added, 'that a heart attack and other afflictions are ruled out in the case of young transgressors.'

MacDonagh proposed that an acknowledged fact be considered. Men had gone up the steps of the gallows with a song on their lips, well contented that the achievement was worth the punishment.

2

THE CASE OF THE TANGLER'S DAUGHTER

Before the advent of the cattle marts and civilisation to Ireland, the country was not ruled by the government, the clergy, the Protestants, the Knights, the Freemasons or Fianna Fáil. No. It was run by a race of men known as tanglers.

The term 'tangler' is used to indicate that human being who was the link between the cattle dealer and the buying or selling citizen. He was at once admired and despised. The tangler was penniless but beholden to his wealthy and mobile employer. Nevertheless, by virtue of his tongue and sales talents, he had the plain farmer vice-gripped by the bags. He had the cattle dealer and rancher gripped by the like extremities. The tangler was motivated by the same urge as the Byzantine eunuch. His talent, wit and tongue were at the service of his overlord, a man he considered not fit to brush a bull's back. This factor made him range from a sweet-talking flatterer to a demon of spite.

I see them now on the fairs in my mind's eye. Brown felt hat, shiny brown boots, a ferruled ashplant, fawn pants, collar, red tie and tie pin, the ensemble covered in a natty gabardine coat, well cut and tailored. They operated in the following manner. Enter cattle dealer and tangler upon site of fair. Cattle dealer approaches small farmer, sheltering his eyes humbly under a peaked cap. Dealer says to farmer, 'God save

14

you, my good man, how much for the little cattle?' Small farmer says, 'Only fifty pounds apiece, sir.' Dealer pretends to take weakness. He staggers and moves away in a state of shock. The tangler shouts at the top of his voice, 'Come back, come back!' and *sotto voce* to small farmer, 'Leave this to me, Jamesy. I'll get you your price.' By noon the little farmer has sold the cattle, the wife, the children and himself into slavery, delighted with the annual privilege.

The second girl I had a notion of was the daughter of a tangler named Tom Boyle, tangler to Mr John Redmond Bowe, a major cattle dealer of Ferrycarrig. She caught my eye. She was full of frolics and had a very nice laugh. What happier association whereby I could learn the trade, see the world and maybe make a few notes for the home place and the mother? In addition I would have the daughter Phyllis's animated prattle and hot cheeks. All in comfort. The place at home was only one jump ahead of the bailiff at the time. I made it up to meet her.

The uncle Dick was mumming at the time with the Drinagh mumming and traditional dance group. I went with him to a mummers' ball at Carcur, where I got in tow with Phyllis. She let me walk home with her that night and introduced me to her daddy. He not only brought me in and gave me a mug of hot milk but also informed me that all belonging to me were decent people, especially the uncle Dick, who would give you his right arm. 'I hope with the help of God you'll take after him and be half as good a man,' he said with a flourish. After that I went with Tom Boyle to the fairs of Wexford, Clonmel, Carrick-on-Suir, Ballybrickan, Taghmon and Castlebridge. I studied his strategy very carefully. Before long I was in a position to persuade the lifebelt off a sailor. I was also playing cards very well and I got to speak the tangler's language with fluency. I would go

15

far in the world was the opinion of Mr John Redmond Bowe, the boss.

The mother had wintered eight little whitehead bullocks on land which grew little more than rushes and rough grass. However, the trade was so brisk that anything that could walk was marketable. There was a hunger on the English for young cattle. 'Nicholas, hon,' she said, 'send Mr Bowe over to me this week until I try his temperature. We'll put the cattle into the small house where they'll look big and will support one against the other, in case any of them take a stagger. A rub of hair oil on their backs to put them in show condition would be no harm either.'

Mr Bowe, the cattle dealer, came over to Mulgannon, and with him my friend and patron, Mr Tom Boyle, the tangler, as bright as a buttercup in corn.

'How much do you want for the eight little bullocks now, ma'am?' asked Mr Bowe politely.

The mother was blowing the fan. She commenced blowing it harder to indicate agitation. The sparks lodged and died on the soot over the hearth. 'I'm a poor widow, Mr Bowe,' she said. 'All I want is fifty-four pounds ten apiece.'

Mr Bowe turned smartly around, like a shot soldier, out through the half-door and up the lane to the car. The tangler let out a screech. 'Come back! Come back here at wanst! The poor little woman is demented over the loss of her husband; she's out of her mind and doesn't know what she's saying! Come back!'

Didn't she know, faith? She asked ten pounds over their value and the eight of them wheezing like concertinas.

Mr Boyle turned to me quickly, then out of the corner of his mouth, 'Are they sound?'

'As sound as the National Bank,' I said, not going to let the mother down.

They came to terms, but Mr Bowe told Boyle that it would be his funeral if anything happened to the cattle for the next seven days. He was referring to their health. They were driven away and put out on fresh grass, a thing their stomachs had no experience of. Two nights later I brought Phylis to see *The Last of the Mohicans* and afterwards I brought her for some fish and chips. We took our time going home.

The Boyle home lay up a hill overlooking a scene of beauty. At this location the broad and pleasant Slaney bursts from its narrows into Wexford's inner harbour and it gurgles between two fortresses, which would laugh at the Rhine's best efforts. As we walked along, with the vista proclaiming the inadequacy of mortal chat, we had peril thrust upon us. There was her father out waiting for us on the road. He had a horsewhip in his hand. I could plainly see him flexing like an unleashed greyhound. His three dogs were all jumping and howling around him, waiting for the word to attack. The prospect was not concerned with the kind word. Boyle's bitter face presiding over the scene confirmed my fear. I stopped dead. He turned to me and addressed me in a half-wail, which started off at a low pitch and went up to sawmill howl.

'Three of them down with the murrin, God blast you. Two of them ett with flukes. Three more rotten with consumption. I will take your sacred life.' He took to run at me, dogs and all. I had to run across the fields like a badger with the dogs at my heels and he making cuts at me with the whip through the frost. This panting man of fifty-eight years of age followed me across country and at one stage his hot breath was on the back of my neck. I turned out of the fields at Carraig graveyard, forded the little river in my best clothes, ran down by the hospital, up to the Windmill Hills, over to Whiterock and across the land to Mulgannon. And

Thomas Boyle, Esquire, plus dogs, only gave up the chase through exhaustion at Whitemill. I fell into our own yard, safe only when greeted by our own dog and the gate locked. Here at last behind our Siegfried Line I could afford impudence. It took me a twenty-four hours to recover.

Phyllis never spoke to me again after that. Her last words to me were, 'You have deceived my daddy. He is made a hunt of before the people.'

The mother had her money, of course, and didn't give a damn.

'Caveat emptor, Mrs Furlong,' the solicitor said.

I often think, looking back on that case, that I was thwarted by the mother.

*

The conclusion of this alarming experience afforded me a distraction of mind, from romance to male companionship. Besides, there were other interests in the world to which I wished to give attention.

I have always been a great man for politics, the international scene no less than the national. This interest stems from a day in the Christian Brothers' second class, when I told my deskmate, Dessie Carroll, that I was up for the British in the war, and who was he up for. He informed me that the British were no good and that he was up for the Germans. I decided that I would be up for the Germans too. From that moment I was never deceived by Mr Churchill's assertion that Britain fought for the freedom of the world, and I was quick to note that if the Germans occupied most of Europe, the British occupied civilisations thousands of miles away like India, Malaya, Egypt, Gibraltar, Burma and Persia, not to mention the Six Counties. I began to collect evidence to support my point of view, by means of newspaper cuttings, which I carefully entered into scrapbooks. If the rest of the world was to be codded, I most certainly was not.

Mr MacDonagh senior, my companion's father, was a meticulous record-keeping man. We often had discussions. He collected the *London Illustrated News*, the *Irish Times*, the *Financial Times*, *Hibernia* and the *Messenger of the Sacred Heart*. Mr MacDonagh was concerned lest the Protestants get the upper hand in business. If a scarce commodity was to be obtained in Wexford, he (Mr MacDonagh senior) noted that it was not the Catholic firms that displayed it, but other parties. He eschewed Fenianism nevertheless. He mentioned his complete collection of the *London Illustrated News* of 1942. I must confess that I was overwhelmed with desire to convert to my own use this most interesting set.

It so happened that I met an impure companion on the fair of Ross during my tuition with Mr Boyle. He gave me a calendar of twelve pages, a page for each month, on each page of which there was an unchaste picture in colour. I brought this to the attention of MacDonagh junior and indicated that he could have same in return for the 1942 issues of the *London Illustrated News*. I allowed him to view Miss January. MacDonagh junior indicated that, much as he would like to oblige me, his father would break every bone in his back. Even a loan would not suffice, for he suggested that I would allow droppings from my porridge to fall on the pages. I pointed out that if that was his attitude it made no odds to me. MacDonagh said that he would return in one hour but stipulated that the exchange would have to be a loan for one week. I was agreeable to this on condition that Mulcahy not be allowed to see the unchaste calendar in case he might turn into a goat.

At this time the mother purchased a van for the sum of one hundred and forty-five pounds from Ibar Maguire in the Rope Walk Yard. There was nothing wrong with it. We brought calves and pigs around in it and I learned how to drive. I wouldn't always be under a compliment to Mulcahy for being driven around in his father's car.

These unconnected matters were destined to play an important role in my life and business.

3

THE BOLD SHELMALIERS

It's a while now since the Shelmalier Young Farmers' Club held an all-night dance in Curracloe and invited members from the whole of Ireland for nothing. I will repeat that, for it is an historic fact. The event was by invitation to Irish members, free. Yet it wasn't because of the new van or because there was no charge that prompted the uncle Dick to propose that he and I attend.

'Come on, my boy. I'll train you how to handle yourself, in case you grow up to be a loon.'

When we got to the door, he gave me a Young Farmers' Club badge to put on and he also put one on himself. 'That,' he whispered, 'is lesson number one, and here, free of charge, is lesson number two: if a girl says she's from the Macamores, fly from her the same as if she had foot and mouth, because the land is so wet that frogs skid on it. It doesn't matter if she's like a film star. Lastly, the best women in the world on all counts come from Castlebridge, and listen here, keep far away from me when I'm doing business but keep your eyes on me, for it's the old dog for the hard road and the pup for the path.'

He gave me a half-crown for lemonade and jumped into the crowd with a raucous, 'Yoo-hoo, Liz! Here I am!'

I kept my eyes on him. At one point I saw him jumping

up in the air for balloons. He had a red paper hat on him, with the colour trickling down off it with every bead of sweat. I thought he'd have taken a seizure.

I was standing sucking my thumbs when over to me strode a bold lassie. 'What do you mean,' she said, as brazen as you like, 'by staring at me like that the whole night?'

At this turn of events I said to myself that I might as well be killed for a sheep as a lamb, so I said to her, 'Because to tell you the truth, miss, I take a fancy to you.'

I had never set eyes on her before but she had shiny black earrings and a gorgeous wave in her hair. As well as these qualifications she had rosy cheeks, a dimple on her chin, an interesting cross look and she was the same size as myself. Almost at once, the MC announced a slow foxtrot. I at once added that I would be most grateful if she would let me dance with her. She replied, 'All right.'

In that jostling mob, any effort at delicacy of step was aborted. We were pressed and rammed together as the dance wore on. She asked me what branch I was on. I replied, 'Piercestown.' I then opened up an exploration of her mind with a very broad question.

'What,' I asked, 'do you like best apart from your work?'

She took a long time to consider this, for she threw me a look. Then she brightened and said, 'Well now, one thing I am very interested in is politics. It's so varied, do you know.'

'Oh,' said I, not too alert. 'Fine Gael, perhaps?'

It was the wrong phrase. At that moment a look of hatred disfigured her face to such an extent that I backed away. I had only seen that open maw of war on one other face, to wit, my parent of the maternal persuasion. This was no time for confusion and I remembered words from a teacher who had disagreed with the appointment of a rate collector.

22

'No,' I said, 'I think you prefer a group which loves its country more.'

That was a fair ball and it went all the way into the net. She smiled happily and rested her hot forehead on mine. The dance finished and I took the precaution to guard her across the room to her place. I said I would be back. As I murdered my way through the throng I saw Richard Furlong following me like a hovering submarine. He came across the hall directly to where I was. He brushed deliberately by me. As he did, he uttered the following words from the side of his mouth: 'That's Black Breen's daughter. Mind yourself.' And he vanished. That was the first time he ever signalled concern for my well-being.

Black Breen's daughter! 'Black Breen', the man who started the civil war in County Wexford. He wasn't known as 'black' because of his hair. He was known as 'black' because when the passion of hate overwhelmed him, his face was known to turn black. Here he was now, a well-off pillar of society, up to the eyeballs in politics, and the local elections coming up. He had thrown in his lot with Clann na Poblachta – which means 'the Family of the Republic' – a group of constitutional revolutionaries. I elected to embark on a bold voyage.

I made it my business to have the very next dance with a gramophone from Oylegate who was in Miss Breen's company. I informed her that I was the winner of the Macra na Feirme gold medal for oratory in the national championships the previous year and that my prize was a tour of Holland. After that particular dance, the gramophone and Miss Breen entered the ladies' room together.

Fortune followed the favoured one. The next dance was a ladies' choice. Who came over to me but my delight.

'What's sauce for the goose is sauce for the gander,' she said. 'Will you dance with me?'

She told me all about herself in the next few minutes. She referred to my prize gained for oratory. 'Perhaps,' she said, 'you have already met Daddy.'

I stood erect and addressed her. 'I have not had that great honour, but who has not envied the many admitted to your father's company, for he is a legend in our land?'

'That was a very nice thing to say,' she said, and followed, with a frown, 'He has not been well and yet he is flogging himself to death in these stupid local elections. I wouldn't mind if there was anything to be got out of it.'

'I would like to help your father in the elections,' I said.

The uncle tottered over to me, a spent carcass imploring exhausted retreat, but I told him to hump off on his own in the van. That night I was left home by the girl, Anastasia Breen of Ballymurn House.

*

The mother was moaning and blowing the fire fan in the corner of the kitchen. There was nothing unusual in that, except there was no fire in the grate.

'Child, child, the breed of that one would flog you to death and laugh at your predicament. When I think of the evictions and your poor grandfather. Is it my Nicholas or have the fairies taken him?' and a long rigmarole like that.

All I did was to paste posters on seven trees requesting the electorate to vote No. 1 for my intended's father: 'VOTE No. 1, DANIEL J. BREEN'. She was bitter in her remarks. I flushed scarlet with temper but said nothing. That was the best way to put manners on the mother.

She stopped blowing the fan and sat bolt upright. She

24

continued in her belligerence, 'The Breens were jumping ten feet into the air with the dint of the hunger fifty years ago until the post-office raids.' The mother slapped her two hands down on her knees. 'And that, Nicholas, is the crowd you've got yourself in with this night. If you make your bed, you'll have to lie on it.'

I didn't give a damn if he was a Bolshevik; I was to be the last speaker at the final election rally in Oylegate that night. I told the people that if Daniel Breen got in, the farmers would get a cash increase per gallon for milk at once. I also lashed out something that I heard off Jimmy O'Dea on the wireless, namely that the harp was the emblem of Ireland because the country was run by pulling strings. Everybody laughed and cheered. My public speech was very well received.

I must confess to unease whenever I was in the house after that election. I was in top gear before and during the elections. I had been received with the red carpet and backslaps. No choice of grub was too much for me, no confidence of a political-defamation nature too private for my ears. I was informed of a most interesting factor by Mr Breen. He claimed that Fine Gael men could be spotted at a hundred yards because of the conniving drop in their eyes.

I laughed and slapped him heartily on the back. 'Well, that's a good one, Mr Breen,' I said, 'because my uncle, Richard Furlong, always looked normal to me, from a political aspect anyhow.' It was at this that I first observed his awful black look. Afterwards I often caught Mr Breen looking at me, and although there had to be a mental explanation for it, I kept noticing the black look. Then he'd take his eyes off me and shake the newspaper straight with unusual vigour. Although not a word was said – indeed, there was a notable absence of words – I started to dislike the conniving old begrudger looking at me as if I was going to steal the complexion off his daughter's cheeks.

I brought her home myself one night, from Curracloe Strand – not that I was in receipt of anything except the stink of seaweed. It was late, after midnight. She told me her father's heart was bad and that he must have his rest. He would be asleep, on pills. I was warned not to wake the greyhounds or make the slightest noise. Daddy was a very light sleeper and, like the dogs, would wake up if a flea let a fart. There were flagged steps up to the hall door and a parapet around the house. Under the parapet were flowers of all kinds under glass. It was so black a night that you could not see your hand.

'Goodnight,' she said. 'I really am very tired and I've a splitting headache.'

It was on the tip of my tongue to tell her there were worse complaints than splitting headaches. I took two backward steps while watching her at the door to indicate concern lest the granite façade collapse around her drawers. I vanished over the parapet.

It was a four-foot drop. My landing from black space was accompanied by a spectrum of sound. There was my own shriek. There was the contiguous crash of twenty panes of glass and their frames. The yowls of the greyhounds followed, with the contributions of every other dog in the parish. Windows shot up with a bang.

'Who the hell is there? I'll take his life!'

'Your heart, Daniel!'

'It's nothing, Daddy.'

Shots discharged. Horses kicking the shit out of timber stalls.

'Where is the bastard? I can't see him.'

More deafening shots.

'Oh heavens, the geraniums!'

'The hoor's melt, where is he?'

But of Nicholas there was so sign, for the fright had put the compass of his mind astray and he clocked ninety in the van past the mill of Garrylough, vowing to Almighty God that he would never set foot in Ballymurn again, even if he were to be made Minister of Agriculture.

4

The Commandments

There wouldn't have been any pass put on the uncle in our house, only he had the name of money. The mother had it in for him because he never lost the chance of giving her the dart about marrying into quality. He came in the door one day, just as she had the kindling lit on top of the griddle.

'God save all here,' he remarked wickedly as he back-heeled the half-door shut.

'Kindly,' the mother said, hoping at the same time that he'd die roaring for the priest.

'Do you know what it is, Kate?' he said, settling himself down over the settee. 'The country is going straight back to the time of the Druids.'

The mother kept blowing the fan. Her shiny county-council glasses were perched on her cocked nose under a grey wisp, and she half-crouched, murmuring, 'Musha, musha.' She looked as harmless as a dandelion, a demeanour the begrudger often mistook for genuine, to his or her cost.

'Listen to this.' The uncle took a newspaper out of his pocket. '"Sunshine Queen of 1952",' he said. '"Parish of Piercestown final, next Friday night." Sunshine Queen, Kate. Last Thursday night, twenty-four brazen trollops went to Camross and paraded around the hall with numbers on their backs, like greyhounds in Shelbourne Park, and they smothered in paint and lacquer, in a Christian country. Are their fathers out of their minds that they don't break shovel handles across their backs?'

The mother looked over her specs and remarked, 'You didn't collect all that information at home over the fire.' She had a fear that he'd go cracked, marry a flapper and leave her every single scut.

The uncle shook the paper in contempt and addressed me. 'You're seventeen or eighteen now, shaving a good while. I hope, my boy, when you are about a wife, you'll look for a good lump of a woman with strong legs fit to carry half a ton of hay across the yard' – a quick glance at the mother – 'and not one of your fol-de-dols.'

He was out the door before she could retort, but the cut had gone home. I wondered if the mother had been one of those beauty queens in her day. I had been over at the table, reading a book she had brought home for me from town. It was *The Life of the Apostle of Temperance Fr Mathew OFM Cap*. I resolved at once that, through fire and water, I'd go to Piercestown Hall the next Friday night.

It was no easy job to whip the van out from under the mother's nose, and it was twice as hard to get it back. We had a big black horse, a kind, agreeable animal. I made arrangements to leave him tied in a paddock the odd night I wanted the van. I would tie jute sacks around the horse's hoofs and yoke him with swing and chain to the van, thus pulling it noiselessly for fifty yards up the road with me at the wheel.

I set out, respectably dressed, with a nice shirt and maroon tie. I didn't tell MacDonagh or Mulcahy. What would be the point in telling those two Jemmies if I was on to a good thing? I had my total-abstinence pin up, as well as the Young Farmers' badge. The girl I was after would need to regard me as one who would not take advantage of her fragility.

There was a lovely sloe-eyed girl there with fair, wavy hair and an attractive silk blouse that you could nearly see through. She had a number in her hand. She told me that she was the entry from Kilmore, by the name of Caitriona Parle. We danced away. 'You've a lovely smile,' she said. 'You should smile more often.'

I asked her if she was idle for the night, addressing her politely as 'Miss'.

'I am,' she said.

'Well, I'd like if I could bring you home,' I gallantly declared.

'Oh,' said she, 'have you transport?'

'I have a brand new van,' I said.

I was very civil because I knew by the signs that I was beginning to dote on her and she on me. That's how it all started.

Caitriona swept all before her. She went through all the competitions in a canter, with the other entrants fit to cut her throat. She won the heats of the competition in Boolavogue, Oulart, Kilmuckridge and Blackwater. Everything was all right until my photo appeared in the paper with my arm around Caitriona, and she with a broad sash around her. 'Miss Galbally 1952' was on it.

The uncle arrived up to the mother with fire in his eyes. 'Will you look at the get-up of that dying whelp, Kate,' he said, producing the paper. 'It wouldn't surprise me if he was taking a sup of the hard stuff on the quiet as well.'

'If he has formed one or the other habit, he didn't pick them up off the ground, for they are in his blood,' the mother said, facing him boldly, bitter at your man's impudence and proud as Lucifer to see my picture in the paper with my name and address correctly spelled.

Then the county final came. It was to decide Miss Sunshine Wexford, an honour which would bring the winner far in the world, with a week free in the Mosney Holiday Camp and a film test in London.

The final was fixed for Courtown Harbour, about thirty-five miles from my base. I kept avoiding Mulcahy and MacDonagh, with their long faces of want on them. But of course Uncle Richard Nobs FitzArsehole MacFurlong threw a spanner in the works. He wanted the van. He put it up to the mother and she gave her consent for the very two days I wanted it for Caitriona and the final. Even if I had asked for it, I wouldn't have got it, for the mother had strong views on girls who exposed themselves in competitions. She said they were common, and expressed the wish that I, Nicholas, would never turn into an old feck.

I mentioned the term 'old feck' a week later to MacDonagh and he volunteered that its meaning described one who before and after accepting the privileges of the married state recited a pious aspiration and an Act of Contrition. Mulcahy took a poor view of MacDonagh's explanation. Be that as it may, there would be no bus for Nicholas and the mott. I was not dismayed, for God never shut one door but he opened another.

I was that fond of Caitriona that I contrived to sell a sow, which was not my property, but was with our own sows for safe keeping as a favour. When the time arose to return the sow to its owner, I could substitute another sow of our own. On the other hand, the related person who deposited the sow into our custody might be so caught up with cultural affairs that he might not miss the sow at all. Having sold the sow, I was in sufficient funds to hire a taxi. I put a dicky bow on myself, too.

You should have seen the talent there that night, along with the different hairstyles, dresses and attitudes of the women. But the opposition cut no ice with Caitriona. What

31

did she do? She put on a mysterious false mole, high on her cheekbone. She walked away with the prize. From that moment, she had great difficulty in spurning the advances of some immaculately dressed Dublin paupers who were attached to the booze factory which sponsored the event.

Things, however, were going on too well to last. I could smell it in the air. I was doing a tango in the victory dance. Who fell out on the floor, maggoty with beer, his lower jaw trembling with rage, only the uncle Dick. He spotted the two of us and advanced like a train.

'I'll give you sow, you feckin' scourge!' he bawled. 'A grand gay little sow that was as quiet as a lamb.'

Dancing ceased; all eyes were on us. He turned eyes on Caitriona. 'Is this the narrow whippet you've hawked around the county in your mother's van?'

The stewards were arriving at speed. The uncle made a box at me and fell up against Caitriona, whereby the brute made a black smear of Caitriona's mole. She flushed scarlet with fury, put her hand over her mole and flounced off, but not before she told me and the uncle we were only guttersnipes and that the whole night was ruined. The stewards carried out the uncle, boxing and shouting, 'Me sow! Me sow!'

I waited for two hours outside the girls' cloakroom but she did not emerge. She must have gone out through a skylight. I never saw her any more. She married a lightship man after, and the best of luck to him. The mother was pleased and told me that Caitriona was only scruff.

*

Shortly after that reverse, there was an awful row with the boys and the several families in Mulgannon. The trouble stemmed from the fact that the mother inherited a horseman along with the family farm. Horseman and ploughman, he was a long, lean liar who thrived on rising disturbances. The horseman in every farm has the privilege of cutting and converting to his own profit the hair off the horses. It was a valuable commodity, used for stuffing horse tackle, sofas and mattresses, and fetched a good few shillings at any saddlery. Moses Flaherty was the horseman's name. (He went by the term of Mosie.) He had a year's horsehair in a bag, hidden where I or no one else could find it – or so he thought.

One day, Mulcahy told MacDonagh and myself that he would bring us to a posh party in New Ross in his own car, on condition that we put in the petrol. At this, MacDonagh began to whinge that he had no money.

'Very well,' said Mulcahy in a superior fashion, 'we'll forget about the whole matter.'

'Ah, shag you, Mulcahy, you lousy shite, you're rotten with money. Why can't you bring the feckin' car? Won't your Da fill her up? What would it be to Ross? Three lousy gallons, and if she wouldn't do it on that she's a heap of scrap,' flooded MacDonagh with teeth stripped.

'It's not a question,' said Mulcahy, 'of whether or not my father will fill the car with petrol. It's a question of principle.'

'What principle, for Jazes' sake?' said MacDonagh.

'The principle of fair play, and if there's any bad language I won't go at all,' replied Mulcahy.

'Bawlze!' screamed MacDonagh.

'I'll put the petrol in the car,' I said in order to stop Mulcahy putting MacDonagh's two eyes into one.

I got thirty-two shillings and sixpence for the horsehair.

The party in New Ross beat the bun. There were fresh girls, schoolgirls, old girls and bold girls. There was drink for everybody who wanted it and dances and games. There was postman's knock and spin the bottle and a game of numbers.

Everyone was given a number, the boys even numbers and the girls odd numbers. A boy started and went outside the door and called out 'Seventeen'. Number Seventeen, whoever she was, then had to go outside the door and kiss the boy. Then it was her turn to call an even number. Of course no one knew which number was which. After half an hour, I had done no business. MacDonagh had been out three times, and took about five minutes each time, until they had to slow-handclap him. One girl said, 'No. Please.' and walked back in before Mac-Donagh, red and furious. She said he was a cur in his heart.

After a long time, one of the finest girls in the place had her number called and she ambled languidly out. She was twenty-eight and engaged to an architect in Cork. She was a sultry and attractive bird. She called 'Twenty-two'. My number. I was numb. There was a cheer from the assembly. I hesitated and MacDonagh gave me a push. I went out into the dark and there she was, with a half-smile, a pearl necklace and a black bulging sweater. I came forward with my hands by my side. She came to me. The perfume was unusual, but evocative of seas and lakes and gardens and the Taj Mahal and girls. She put her arms around me and asked, 'Are you Nicky?'

I said, 'Yes.'

She ran her slender fingers through my hair and moved my head towards her warm and moist mouth. She closed her lips on mine and sucked mine gently. Then she opened my lips ever so gently with her silver tongue and she slipped it between my teeth and trembled my own tongue with fire and soft sweet surging pressed and withdrawn currents of nuclear delight. She pressed my back with her hand, up and down. Then, as if spent, she slipped her tongue from me, gave herself a quick wipe and also me. She squeezed my hand and said, 'Goodbye, Nicky love, you're very soft.'

I called Number Nineteen. Whoever it was came and went and I knew not who it was. I cared not who it was because I was in a daze from the world I had passed through, a world of softness and magic and unbelievable honey sensation that was only capable of being sustained for a few moments in a lifetime. When I walked back into the glare of the light there was a cheer again. Remarks such as 'Not a scratch on him' and 'What did you do to the girl?' only smote my ears in a dream.

The game was over. Another dance. I sat down and didn't speak, for I couldn't, and she neither spoke to me nor took any notice of me for the rest of the night. Mulcahy and MacDonagh could not encourage a remark or opinion from me either. MacDonagh said that I was the victim of carnal examination. I was really in long consideration of the warm glow and the music and the fun and the affection and all the while recoiling with horror from the prospect of the shit slop and furze bushes, the scouring calves and scuthery chaff, the stinking sows and Mosie Flaherty and the mother the next day on the gale-swept moon craters of Mulgannon where the winter drawers would be blown off you, not to talk of a sprongful of hay from your back. Oh, merciful Jesus, take me.

*

Moses Flaherty soon found that the horsehair was missing. Mulgannon's Moses S. Holmes also decided who the culprit was. His gob was white with rage. 'You lousy hoor, robbing the unfortunate working man, you're no better than all belonging to you, if you saw shit you'd long for it, the curse of God on you,' he said, exploiting that vulgarity of expression so frequently found in people of his station.

'Ah, leave me alone, for feck's sake, all I got was ten

shillings. I was in a jam. I'll pay it back to you,' I said.

'You will; that was the mark of all the Furlongs – they were all that big-hearted; Jazes, it's an awful thing to be poor; they'd shit on you.'

'You've more money than I have, I haven't the price of a smoke. All I have is 10 bob a week. Where would you get with that? The boys had no money either.'

'Aye, two more fair good things; three gets going around the country tearing the knickers off every cross-bred bitch and if ever there's one of them brought in here, I'll have to bend the knee and say "Ma'am". I will in my arse. If your father were alive he'd shit himself. But I'll put a stop to all this carry-on, mark my words.'

He went off muttering to himself, leaving me to ponder this threat. I was never able to foretell from what end the retaliatory attack would come, for Moses Flaherty had a dangerous ration of brains. Going straight up to the mother and blowing the gaff would be far too simple for him. Why pull the pin out of a hand grenade when you can build a time bomb? Moses Flaherty was an accomplished disturbance-riser who gave the impression that he was privately on everyone's side. He had the ear and confidence of every woman in Mulgannon. He waited for about seven days and one day, after dinner, he pushed open the door unexpectedly on the mother.

'God save you, ma'am, it's very harsh.'

The mother straightened herself up with a quizzical frown and said nothing beyond fixing her glasses up high on her nose, thus intimating that she was prepared to listen.

'I heard a little thing down the road, ma'am.'

The mother knew her man, of course. She said nothing but took a step nearer and put her two hands on her hips.

'I heard tell it was boasted in a certain big house, before

the priest collecting the dues, that the only boy to finish out his exams as a college-educated boy was Master Mulcahy and that it was a pity that the rest of the people in Mulgannon didn't think it would be worthwhile educating theirs.'

The feathers on the back of the mother's neck bristled instantly, but of her inner conflict she gave no sign. Putting her head on one side and smiling knowingly, she looked across at me, putting jam on my bread.

'Ah yes, Moses Flaherty,' she said, 'Nicholas could have been college-educated too if he had been reared on margarine. Of course, you don't have to explain Mulgannon to me. I've been through it all. I well remember children coming in here to play with Nicholas, hungry and covered in vermin. On one poor child I cracked two fleas as big as cockroaches. Of course, charity bids me hold my tongue. Be off with you now, Moses Flaherty, before I say more, and don't be coming to me with your cock-and-bull stories.'

Before midnight, her precise words were repeated in the seven households. The following day all hell broke loose and spread across the plateau of Mulgannon. There were visits by women to one another. Charges and counter-charges. Sugar and cash borrowed for threshings at the time of the Boer War were dragged up, as well as watered whiskey, attempted rape, the half-paid man, lunacy, boycotts, debts and watered milk. The corpses of neighbours buried by the State, or by a well-heeled neighbour – who only for his charity would be rich today – were unearthed. Every child or adult who died in decline or consumption was clothed with the stigma of starvation. The whole lot fell on top of the mother and me. A strong rearguard action was fought, but the mother knew she was trapped, because of Mosie Flaherty's lies. I had to defend Flaherty from the mother because if she ate him alive he'd tell her about the horsehair.

And if that woman turned on me, it would be Christ help me.

It was the luck of God that for the four weeks of conflagration that followed there was no trespass by man or beast, for if there had been, the entire population of Mulgannon would have ended up in the District Court. Time is a great healer, but Moses Heartscald Flaherty had the satisfaction of seeing the spectacle of seven houses, the inhabitants of not one of which were speaking to the others. The return from Mass on Sunday up the Mulgannon road resembled the procession of seven sections of the Confraternity separated from one another by twenty yards.

The tidal waves from Mosie Flaherty's revenge continued to scourge. Father George O'Brien, a large stout man, bald, with rimless pince-nez glasses, was the parish priest. He had a booming voice, which could be heard all over the church. He was a great preacher. One Sunday, as the row petered out, he had the eleven o'clock Mass, which most of us attended. After the Gospel and the notices, he took off his watch, wound it, placed it before him, blew his nose into a large white handkerchief and chose the following text for the congregation: "'Woe to the man by whom scandal cometh. It were better for *that man* (pause) to have a millstone tied around his neck and be cast into the depths of the sea.'" (Long pause. Father George adopted an attitude of confidence-sharing and rested his elbow calmly on the pulpit.)

'These, my dearly beloved, are strange times. These latter days are different from the days that your fathers and mothers knew, and that I knew. For these are the days when the polite word is used instead of the dirty word, when common permission is given in our daily talk for crimes that years ago would have caused shock and dismay throughout the land. The man who sold tea and white bread at black-market prices was a businessman. The employer who will not pay his men a just wage is, we are told, an entrepreneur. The foul-mouthed blackguard is regarded as a wit, the discovered thief as unlucky, (an angry roar) the fornicating young devil as the boyfriend *and the bastard as a love child!*'

This roar of thunder sucked silence from the packed church. The only activity it did not stop was the clack of beads, quick-moving mouths and nodding heads of pious women saying their private rosary as if they didn't know what he was talking about. It was clear now, however, that a carnal atrocity had been perpetrated on or by a parishioner in recent days.

'The scandal of the roads at night around the town is not the worst we have to face, although it is the start from which all others flow. Forgive me if I scandalise innocent ears but I am concerned with the man who brought a woman to the altar (roars) *and one woman only!* I am alarmed at the broken homes, the deserted wives, the abandoned children, and yes, let me say it, the drunken sluts who would pawn the bread from an infant's mouth and drink the proceeds.'

He became calm again, almost pleasantly chatting.

'From whom and from where have these pestilences come? From whom, the flood of evil literature?' (A wheezy cough from MacDonagh.) 'Who has sought to lead the young, the uninformed, the innocent, into ways of sin in public and private which years ago would have merited the cat-o'-nine-tails? Here we have no coloured word, no polite word, no nice word; here we have the word which crosses the span of two thousand years and (softly) what is that word, my dearly beloved people?' (A mighty roar) *'The scandalgiver!'* (A contemptuous wave of the hand and continued roar) 'Oh don't tell me I'm old-fashioned! Don't tell me that stuff was all right years ago! Don't tell me there's no such thing! I'll tell you where they are. I'll point them out. The purveyor of pornographic literature (a wheezy cough from MacDonagh). The writer who writes, the blackguard who instructs the youth, the suggestive gesture, the man who can't control his passions and the voluptuary who knows how to kindle them!'

He became incoherent at the knowledge of some awful sin known but to himself and to the transgressors. For a trice his jowls went a-blub a-blub a-blub until his tongue could fashion still-inadequate words.

'Ah, yes, my dearly beloved,' he hissed, 'far, far better for a girl to be kissed by a serpent.' (At this MacDonagh and I gave a salvo of coughs.) 'The woman who reveals the hidden sin of a neighbour, the lewd commercial traveller, the publican who thinks more of the profit than the starving children, the exploiter of the workers . . . Of all these, who can compare with that professor of vice, the man learned and cunning in the nurturing of sin?'

At five minutes to twelve the congregation came out, more dead than alive. The mother said nothing, I said nothing, but Moses Flaherty scooted across the chapel yard and gave the mother a nudge. 'Sore darts there today, ma'am,' he said. The mother scudded on, muttering to herself. The sermon had instigated in her a destabilising process.

*

'You're going to Confession,' the mother said. 'You heard what the priest said on Sunday. You're going now and that's all about it. I won't have you on my conscience and face your dead father after my time. How well you're able to make arrangements for dances, and you won't attend a Holy Hour.'

It was the same all over, as I found out that night when I met Mulcahy and MacDonagh. MacDonagh had Mulcahy out of his mind before the night was over. He reached in under his coat and produced a book he had borrowed from his father's study. It was called *Satan in Society or Before Marriage and After* by a doctor – Nicholas Francis Cooke, MD, LLD, who died at Rhode Island in the United States on 1 February 1885 in the odour of sanctity. He was known as the 'beloved physician'. MacDonagh directed our attention to a passage dealing with sins committed with one's person. He read distinctly from the book. On occasion he would raise his head, pause and look at Mulcahy.

"'At first glance the sinner in privacy presents an aspect of languor, weakness and thinness. The countenance is pale, sunken, flabby, often leaden, or more or less vivid, with a dark circle around the sunken eyes, which are dull or lowered or averted. A sad, shameful, spiritless physiognomy. Sometimes the body is bent, and often there are all the appearances of pulmonary consumption or the characteristics of decrepitude, joined to the habits and pretensions of youth."

'In other words,' said MacDonagh, 'you'd be no worse off than if you fell into the drum of a threshing set and were deposited in shit on the straw rick.'

'Hair is supposed to grow on the palm of the hand of such a sinner,' I volunteered.

Mulcahy said nothing, but a brooding frown sculptured his mug.

'Read on, for the Lord's sake,' I urged.

MacDonagh continued.

"'Consider now this inbruted and degraded being; behold him bent under the weight of crime and infamy, dragging in darkness a remnant of material and animal life. Unfortunate! He has sinned against God, against Nature, and against himself. He has violated the laws of the creator, has disfigured the image of God in his own person and has changed it into

41

the image of the beast (*'imago bestiae'*). He is even sunken lower than the brute, and like him, only looks upon the ground. His dull and stupid glance can no longer raise itself towards heaven. He descends little by little into death, and a last convulsive crisis comes at length, violently to close this strange and horrible drama", the unfortunate poor bollix,' concluded MacDonagh.

'I think it would be in order to go to the Friary,' said Mulcahy.

'I think you're right,' said MacDonagh.

In case this book falls into the hands of heathens, it would be well to point out that the confessing of one's grievous offences humbly and in self-accusation to another mortal man is one of the great consolations of the Orthodox, Roman Catholic and High Anglican religions.

However, all this is very fine in theory. In actual fact, confessors themselves had different approaches. There were easy priests and hard priests – priests who said 'Very good' or 'Good boy' after every confessed sin, priests who looked up to heaven and said 'My God!' and priests like some of the Redemptorists, who give the parish retreats. They would light on you from all angles, particularly about sins antagonistic towards chastity. They had the wind up the parish, with women going mental, or swearing never to see their boy-friends again until they were in a position to get married.

But there was an escape from the lash of a Redemptorist's tongue. The friendly sons of St Francis also heard confessions, and warm humanity was their facility.

The next Saturday night we assembled together and made for the Friary, to pacify our mothers. It was dark when we went up to the Friary and across the yard by Father Corrin's chestnut tree.

A frightening event took place as we approached the

porch. The door swung open and out came a gigantic Friar with a howling, dirty-looking terrier by the scruff of the neck. The Friar was over six feet in height, with grey, wavy hair, glasses and a long jaw, through which a sepulchral voice rumbled forth, from somewhere down in his belly. 'Do you boys own this dog?'

'No, Father,' we answered promptly.

With that, he dropped the dog on the concrete and gave it the greatest root in the ribs of all time that sent it off yowling in a shower of barks.

'The House of God is not to be turned into a kennel,' he rumbled and he tore back into his confession box.

'That's one clergyman I won't go to,' wheezed MacDonagh.

'He's a clergyman I wouldn't like to get on the wrong side of,' I remarked.

'Come on,' said Mulcahy, 'until we get it over with.'

There were six confessionals in the church and outside five of them there was a line of waiting penitents. At the sixth confessional there was no queue at all. There was a quota of women doing pious practices such as the Stations of the Cross, or reciting the rosary while seated. They spotted every stir in the church and our entry was not effected without inward comment. There was over all a smell of incense and waterproof coats and perfume and powder. Having sized up the situation, we made like bullets for the confessional which had no queue, in the belief that speed was the man's forte. It was probably an old doting friar at the end of his days and half asleep. I very shortly discovered that this was not an accurate appraisal of the situation.

The legend over the confessional indicated that the occupant was Father Calisanctus OFM. Mulcahy elected to go first. MacDonagh produced a coin, indicated the harp. A short toss and he went in as number two penitent on the other side, leaving me out in the church to initiate the careful examination of conscience. It was then that certain characteristics of the confessor became apparent. As the slide moved back between the priest and Mulcahy, there was a sound from the confessor of a small muted aeroplane taking off, a song of sound almost like the beginning of a chant.

'Eeeeehhhhow long, son, since your last Confession, mumble, mumble, mumble, biz, biz, biz, biz?' Followed by Mulcahy's faint whisper, whisper, whisper. Cough from priest.

'Mumble, mumble *there were four?*' in a loud, clear voice. Father Calisanctus had the fashion, in the middle of the Confession, of raising his voice and releasing two or three words in loud tones before reverting to his original mumble, mumble. These two or three words could be heard yards from the confessional. It was a matter of concern for the penitent at what stage the confessor decided to broadcast his two or three words.

'Mumble, mumble, mumble, biz, biz, biz, biz,' from Mulcahy. A cough from Father Calisanctus. 'Yes?'

'Mumble, mumble, mumble, mumble, mumble, mumble, biz, biz, biz, biz, biz, biz,' from Mulcahy.

Prolonged low mumbles and 'God bless you' from Father Calisanctus, followed by banging of slide one and the opening of the opposite slide to admit MacDonagh the sinner to the tribunal of penance. Before Mulcahy stepped out of the half-open door, he caught my eye, drew his finger across his throat and walked off. I got up off my knees and went into the vacant side of the confessional.

MacDonagh carried on his wheezy biz, biz, biz, biz, biz, biz, biz, biz, and a long duel of mumbles with Father Calisanctus. Of course MacDonagh knew the score by now and he was shagged if Father Calisanctus was going to raise his voice at any destructive moment. Ah no, MacDonagh would see to that, because he was so crafty he'd herd cats through a gap. He was on to a loser. In the midst of all the mumbles the loud voice announced: 'Hah! Another girl destroyed.' Mumble, mumble, mumble. Angry mumbles from MacDonagh: mumble, mumble, mumble.

He was in for ten minutes, then his slide was shut and mine was opened. At the other side of the gauze I detected a large bald man with glasses and a white handkerchief as big as a sheet. He bent his ear over to me. He moaned a whisper.

'How long?'

'Bless me, Father, for I have sinned; it's two months since my last Confession.'

I had evolved a strategy of sin-telling. I thought it best to tell the lightest sins first.

'I said no morning prayers.'

'All right.'

'I lost my temper several times every day.'

'All right.'

'I struck a cow with a hay-fork.'

'The poor dumb beast.'

'I cursed and blasphemed several times every day.'

Father Calisanctus sat bolt upright in his seat.

'Son, what's blasphemy?'

'It's a sort of curse, Father.'

'What sort of a curse?'

'I don't know exactly.'

'And yet you've confessed that you've blasphemed. To blaspheme, child, is to curse God Almighty Himself several times every day – one of the worst sins you could commit. Did you curse God Almighty Himself several times every day?'

'I surely did not, Father.'

Long silence.

After the above exchange, my voice sank several staves from fright.

'I stole a quantity of horsehair.'

'Horsehair?'

'Yes, Father.'

'Extraordinary! Horsehair! Did you steal it from a poor man or a rich man?'

'Well, I didn't really steal it, in a way. It was horsehair cut off our horses at home, but it is the horseman's, as a custom. He has more money than I have, Father.'

Silence.

'Did you have your parents' permission?'

'No, Father.'

'Give the unfortunate man every penny of that back. Anything else?'

I was steering into deeper waters now. 'I had bad thoughts every day.'

'You thought perhaps you would throw yourself out a window? Or burn your neighbour's house? Or steal a cow, perhaps, or stab yourself with a carving knife?'

'No, Father.'

'These are bad thoughts. What you mean to say, I think, is that you took deliberate pleasure in impure thoughts every day.'

'Yes, Father.'

'How many times roughly?'

'About three times.' Pause. 'Maybe more than that.'

'Are you gainfully employed? Do you work on your farm?'

'Yes, Father.'

'Aye! Anything else?'

'I got a calendar of impure pictures from a man and I looked at that several times for the sake of pleasure every day.'

'Would you like your sister or mother to see you drooling over those pictures?'

'I have no sister.'

'Would you like your mother to see you drooling over those pictures?'

'No, Father.'

The last was an understatement. Since the English language does not provide for answering in the negative in a more emphatic manner, it had to suffice.

'Where are the pictures now?'

If he had heard MacDonagh's Confession he must surely have known that he had them, unless he concealed the sin.

'I gave them to a friend.'

Silence.

'Get them back from your friend at once and burn them! Do you hear me now?'

'Yes, Father.'

'Anything else?'

'Yes.'

'Go on, then.'

My heart was in my mouth.

'You see, I was at this party in a house and there was a game with girls. In the game I kissed five girls.'

'Were they sinful, passionate kisses or were they affection-ate kisses?'

'With one girl the kisses were passionate and with the four other girls they weren't any sort of kisses.'

Here the holy man's patience and silence simultaneously expired. He gave birth to a booming loud oration which bent the candle flames in St Anthony's chapel at the other side of the church. Preceded by a ritual moan, the voice rose in pain, separating each word with a short pause.

'Were – there – *indecent – touches?*'

A barely audible 'No, Father' from me.

'Anything else?'

'No, Father, I think that's all.'

'Well, thank God for that, anyhow. Now, son, listen here to me. The devil finds work for idle hands and idle minds to do. You will have to watch yourself or you'll end up badly, a very easy thing to do. Interest yourself in a hobby or a game. Have you a hobby?'

'Yes, Father, I collect scraps from newspapers and magazines and paste them into books.'

'Scraps of an immoral character?'

'No, Father.'

The Father drew his white handkerchief across his brow, removed and wiped his glasses. 'I take it you have no intention of getting married.'

I was sort of nettled by this. 'I have every intention of getting married but I have been let down several times, through no fault of my own.'

This seemed to interest him immensely and, for once, I felt I was not an anonymous penitent. He withdrew from peering out through the curtain, bent himself into a ball and said with great intent, 'Plenty of time for that matter yet, child. You're young. And I'm going to tell you this, watch your step. Many a boy thought he had married an angel from heaven. By herrings, he soon found out his mistake, ha ha, faith.'

I began to respect the wisdom of this man but time was up and he resorted to his customary words, issued, I presume, to the likes of me.

'Avoid these things: evil literature, bad companions, dangerous occasions of sin. For your penance you are to come in here and say the rosary once, on your own. Not the family rosary, but on your own. You'll be all right if you'll take precautions. The evil companion – yes, watch that. Go frequently to the sacraments. God bless you.'

Slide slammed across. I was in blackness, but it was over. I opened the door of the confession box and blinked out into the glare of the lighted church. I could feel every pious old rip and a few who knew my mother looking at me. They had timed me in the box, no doubt. There too, sitting bolt upright, staring at me with pious expressions were Mac-Donagh and Mulcahy. Mulcahy looked long at his wristwatch. I wasn't worth tuppence and I could feel the women saying, 'There they are now, the curs of holy Ireland.'

When I felt my way outside into the yard, I told Mac-Donagh that he'd have to give me back my immodest calendar. He informed me that he could not do this in conscience, as it would be a dangerous occasion of sin to me. He solemnly undertook to destroy the calendar himself, personally.

Moses Flaherty came to me across the yard the next day. 'I heard you were in to Confession with the man that was out foreign. How did you like him?'

I did not lower my dignity by replying.

'He's the man for youze, three trickadaloobs going around after women, be hell, with the chests bit off them with flays. That's the man to put manners on the likes of youze. Out foreign for years in the war with the Abyssinians and the Japs and the soldiers in the army. Be God he'd want to be.'

I decided to delay paying Moses Flaherty restitution as long as I possibly could.

5

THE KNAVE OF HEARTS

The uncle was a great man for sticking his snot where it wasn't wanted.

'It's time, Kate, and long beyond time, that that galoot was looking ahead for a good woman and not a thackeen.'

'Put more furze on the griddle now, Richard Furlong,' the mother said.

'Do you hear me talking to you, woman? In a short few years there's no one will have the crooked little fecker for love or money. A good woman would do a turn about the place, maybe bring in a few pounds. I often heard that the best combination in the world is a good woman and a useless man.'

'Nicholas is only a big child and I want him to have a bit of fun for himself before he is haltered and plagued by a woman. He's not going to make the mistake that I made. And,' the mother added, nastily enough, 'if he is crooked itself, he didn't get that from me or mine.'

'A big child is right,' the uncle said bitterly, 'and he on the road to Killinick every night of the week to a parcel of wasters. You're not right in the head.'

The uncle didn't come down in the last shower. It wasn't for sight of the mist rising off the Slob that I forced the pedals of a bike up the railway bridge at Killinick, but I'd better give the reasons in chronological order.

Mulcahy was on a hurling team known as the Erin Hopes, in Wexford town. He was the captain and full-back of the junior team. As juniors went, they were light but they were crafty. They had won the minor county final four times in a row due to the genius and generalship of a veteran called Charlie Fitzgerald. Charlie was wind-red in the face and drank to excess from frustration. He wore a cap down over eyes which swivelled with cuteness. He chain-smoked but was as deaf as a post. This accounted for his success, because no one could argue with him. Contrary opinions had to be written down.

I wasn't exactly a star hurler where actual matches were concerned. This was due to two factors. I was short of being big and I was nervous of pain or injury to my person. But at the same time I was a nifty ball player. This account will be without MacDonagh because he wasn't fit to hurl the flies off cowshit, but Mulcahy was another kettle of fish. Gentlemanly and courteous off the field, when he donned the Hopes' jersey he turned into an Antichrist. Indeed, it was often mooted that whenever the Hopes were meeting a big dirty team of bogmen, Mulcahy should be brought onto the pitch in a cage with several tormentors provoking him with hot iron bars. The cage door should then be unlocked to release Mulcahy the instant the whistle went.

Mulcahy called up for me. He said, 'Good evening, Mrs Furlong. Is Nicholas in, please?'

'Oh Nicholas,' the mother called. 'Mr Mulcahy is here for you, come at wunce.'

Nothing used to drive me out of my mind more than listening to insane women with notions and arse-lickers calling Mulcahy 'Mr Mulcahy' because he had the name of money. The other thing that tormented me was to hear the oversized constipation call me 'Nicholas'.

I thrust myself out the door in sullen demeanour. 'What do you want?'

'There's manners for you,' the mother said. '"What do you want?" Isn't that lovely, Mr Mulcahy?'

Mulcahy smiled in a refined manner. 'Nicholas must be in bad humour tonight, Mrs Furlong.'

'Indeed, if you ask me, Mr Mulcahy, Nicholas is in a bad humour every night this while back. My goodness, I do not know what I shall do with him, I really do not,' the mother said, putting on airs.

I glowered at Mulcahy and with a gesture of my head I got him to follow me out of the door to the road before he succeeded in putting me out of my mind.

'What do you want, God blast you?' I asked.

'A favour, Furlong, a favour, no more,' said Mulcahy with hands raised as if subduing an orchestra. 'Your club needs you.'

'Do they? For what?'

'Danger Browne has the flu, I fear, and will not be fit for the replay with the Fintans. Charlie Fitz says you're the man for corner-forward and he has a little function for you to perform.'

The St Fintan's wore green jerseys and were picked from a wide area around the village of Killinick. Their ages varied from twenty-two to forty-two. They believed themselves to be the custodians of the pure tradition of hurling. In contrast, the Wexford-town-based Erin Hopes were regarded as hair-oil men for the most part, fortified by Mulcahy, who had every prospect of being an intercounty full-back. In the first game of the County Wexford Junior Hurling Championships, the Erin Hopes, to the astonishment of the civilised world, succeeded in drawing with the Fintans by a last-minute goal, and two further points from frees conceded by a surprised defence.

No sane student of the game gave Erin Hopes a God's prayer of success in the replay, especially with Danger Browne off. He played at corner-forward and he was big and dirty. The latter word does not refer to his hygienic habits. It refers to a gambit employed by him. His forte was to upset the goalman's nerves. He accomplished this feat whenever the first ball of the game went into the goalmouth parallelogram. He would follow the ball but ignored it. Instead he proceeded to wrap the goalkeeper around the goalpost without detection. This had a considerable unnerving effect on the goalkeeper, who for the rest of the match had to watch Browne in addition to the ball.

I told Mulcahy that I appreciated the club's confidence and would cooperate with the mentors. I attended the club meeting that night, which was held in the Swan Square. Charlie Fitzgerald produced the selected team, which was written down in pencil on the back of a Woodbine cigarette box.

	Hayes	
Cogley	Mulcahy	Dake
Ferguson	Nolan	Cunningham
Butler	Frayne	
Moran	O'Connor	Hughes
Furlong	Sinnott	Colfer

Subs: Doyle, Hutchison, Kelly, Conboy, Rooney, Dempsey

There was murder. Doyle, the first sub, described Mr Fitzgerald as 'a stupid bothered auld flute' when he found me listed as corner-forward. Mr Fitzgerald, being deaf, was immune to all verbal attacks but he was not without perception.

'I don't want no arguments from no one. If you hurl as well as you give lip, we're home and dried. I'll give the orders.'

Looking back on the event, one thing is clear. I was selected by Charlie Fitzgerald because I was expendable, and it didn't matter to the club or the country if I was killed or maimed during the course of the game.

'There are two things in my mind,' said Fitzgerald. 'The Fintans' goalkeeper would stop jar taws. He'll have to be got shut of. There's no Browne, so he's going to go out on the field without the fear of God on him. As well as that, they've got a dark horse. They're bringing on a Kilkenny man named Ned Grace from the customs and excise in Rosslare. I have it for gospel. He's going in at centre-back and he played for Kilkenny four years ago. I'll give you your final instructions before the match. I want to see you all here sharp on Sunday after twelve Mass. One other thing – if anyone asks you, say we're going to be hurled out of it. We're going to be no such thing. We'll rattle the turnips in them.'

The latter remark refers to the widely held belief among town teams that teams from the country play after eating a feed of turnips for the noonday dinner.

The Hopes hadn't a hope. Still, there was no excuse for Sean Gilroy's paragraph in the *Wexford Free Press*.

HOPES SELECTORS DEPRESS

It is a matter of some astonishment to have to discuss next Sunday's junior hurling replay between St Fintan's and the town-based Erin Hopes.

The last-minute equalising scores by the Hopes were as much a source of wonder to the Hopes as to the Fintans. Though there may have been a miscarriage of justice, one cannot cavil at the manner in which the Hopes persevered to snatch the vital five points at the call of time. It is therefore with dismay that the town supporters viewed the Hopes' selection for the replay.

Gone is D. Browne through illness. Dake, a forward, is placed in the full-back line and Frayne is brought to centre-field. It is, however, in the full forward line that panic seems to have seized the selectors. To replace the impetuous Browne at corner forward, the Hopes bring on an immature player who hitherto was not even named as a sub. N. Furlong replaces Browne at corner-forward and the industrious Doyle remains on the substitutes' bench – not to speak of the five others. Augmenting an already impressive St Fintan's back division is former Kilkenny centre-back and now Rosslare-based Edmund Grace of Dualla. It would be an abuse of the intelligence of the Wexford hurling public to suggest that the Erin Hopes will survive the first half of the replay with hope undiminished.

The mother said that every mother's son of the Gilroys were besters. The effect of his remarks, however, was a remarkable uplift in the morale of players and supporters from the Swan Square. The mothers and girlfriends, sisters and brothers, uncles, aunts and fathers of everyone who had ever donned the black and white of the Hopes turned up. As we raced out, visible and jumping, onto Wexford Park on a dry, sunny day, there was a roar from a thousand blood relations and hundreds of sympathisers.

'Rattle the turnips in 'em!'

'We never feared yiz!'

'Come on, the Hopes!'

I was in good form. The mother threw holy water on me and gave me a Sacred Heart badge to keep me from all hurt and harm. She wouldn't go to the match in case anything happened to me, and she only having the one. Charlie Fitzgerald was out sucking Woodbine butts. Mulcahy was working himself up into a neurotic state to be channelled later into clatters to the Fintans' forwards. There was bad blood between the country team and the town. Fitzgerald called me over before I went out.

'Come here,' he said. 'You have one job today. One job, and nothing else. Never mind the ball. They all think you're a bag of wind and that's the way to have it. Stay near the sideline for the first ten minutes. Make out that you're only a gom who doesn't know one end of a hurl from the other. Pass foolish remarks to the corner-back, Tom Rowe. Let him walk on you a couple of times. After about fifteen minutes, he'll be changed up to the attack. They'll send a turnip-masher like Gumza Brady to mark you. Give him his way for a few minutes. Then the next time the ball lands in the square, go in and massacre the goalman. If you haven't wrecked him properly and he's still in the goal, keep passing remarks – "There's county-council cottage for you" or "There's another roof slate" or "There's the shithouse". He was turned down for a council house last week, and he on the Feena Fall party. Shout "Up Dev" every now and again. And don't be afraid of him. He's only your size. The rest of the backs will have no pass on you. They think you wouldn't burst balloons. Show them what you're made of – Mulgannon diesel on fire.'

Charlie gave my arm a squeeze, winked in confidence and said, 'Up the Hopes.'

I trotted out onto the field, prepared to maim Grace himself if it came to that, for the honour of the black and white. The man who was marking me was a fat block of a muscleman named Tom Rowe. He tried to put voodoo on me from the start by trying the spring in his hurley and shaving grass with cuts of an imaginary ball. Then he started spitting on his hands, flexing his arms and staring at me with a dead stare. I remarked that it was a nice day for the game if the weather held out, please God. The only retort to my remark was, 'Go away from me, you drink of water.'

At the advent of the first ball from the air, he made room for himself by swishing the hurl over his head and making cuts in the air and grunts like: 'Come ou' a that, come ou' a that.' I made a few pokes at the ball and fell back off his shoulder onto the ground. He made a ground-devouring clearance, which was accompanied by much cheering and huzzas from the bogmen. Thereafter, whenever the ball landed, Rowe allowed himself additional stylish touches and sidesteps which won the heart of the crowd. One jeer wanted to know when my time was up to farrow – a rustic essay at humour which brought boisterous laughter from the yokels.

Then every word that Charlie Fitzgerald prophesied came to pass. The score at the end of the first quarter was: St Fintan's, one goal and five points; Erin Hopes, three points (all from frees). It meant that, despite a Fintans superiority, we were still within striking distance, and the Fintans had lost at least one chance of a goal. The crowd began to roar to bring Rowe up the field. This was done to acclamation, and lo, Gumza Brady was sent back to mind me, a task which was not going to be too hard in his estimation, no doubt. The Fintans' backs, reinforced by Grace, went to pains to keep the other five forwards out, off the goalie. On the three occasions that there was a breakthrough, he brought off

57

dazzling saves, and after one dispatch of play showed the ball to our Johnny Hughes before he cleared. That was tempting God.

Shortly after, Gumza Brady remarked to me that you'd want to be in the best of your health for this game – the implication being that I wasn't. The score stood at 2–6 to 6 points, against us. There remained five minutes of play before the end of the first half. A harmless lobbing ball came in from centre field, which drew out the confident full-back and also my marker, Gumza Brady. Our full-forward, Jim Sinnott, cracked it across smartly between me and the goalkeeper. The goalkeeper was taking no risk pursuing the ball with only me to beat. The day, the hour, the moment of denouement had arrived.

I ran into the goalie with a hunch at speed and a belt in the heart that rattled every tooth in his head: the goal was empty but a Fintans back went in to cover off. However, I now had the ball in my hand and no black-hearted cur to hurt me. I picked my spot and lashed the ball in with every ounce of fury I could summon. The net went up like a flak explosion. Up with the green flag for a goal.

Pandemonium: hats, yells of defiance, colours, the lot. 'There's "child" for you,' bawled Charlie Fitz.

The ball was pucked out in silence. It returned immediately from our Butler to the opposite wing from me. Hughes nabbed it and lashed in a fierce daisy-cutter. Before it hit the back of the net I was on the goalkeeper's back accompanied by three other Hopes forwards. I knocked him with a slap full force against the corner post, shouting, 'There's council house for you!' and I marked my boots on him on the way out.

The last I saw of him was his tongue hanging out and gulping great scoopfuls of air, flat on the ground, and the curate of Ballymore–Mayglass, Father Corish, calling for a stretcher. This time there were no more shouts about sows farrowing, but yells of 'Put him off!' and 'Beeoooooooo!' from the aboriginals. The half-time whistle went and in we trooped, contented men. Doyle wanted me taken off because I'd done my job. But no, Charlie Fitz thought. He sucked his Woodbine. 'The writing is on the wall,' he prophesied. He knew from then on I'd be a marked man and that attention would be diverted from the other five forwards.

When we came out of the dressing room for the second half, I could see the beady eyes of the whole Fintans team upon our Nicholas. Grace loped over by way of no harm and bent his long frame to rest over his hurley.

'I've my eye on you. I'll wipe the laugh off your face before long more, my cute, underhanded, conniving badger's bollocks.'

'I don't see the goalman,' I replied. 'Has he gone home?'

No, the goalman had not gone home, but had refused to come out, and there was internecine strife in the Fintans' dressing room at half-time, for he blamed the whole back line for cowardice in not protecting his body from the multiple bruises of which he was now in unhappy possession.

The new Fintans' goalie wouldn't stop a haystack, and conceded two goals that any grandmother with a wide skirt would save. Panic set in. Nothing went right for them. At the start of the third quarter I found myself in an unmarked position outside our half-forward, Johnny Moran, who was in possession. I let a screech at him. 'The ball! Gimme the ball, the ball!'

He clipped the ball across to me and I closed my fist on it. The next thing, I got an airborne volley in the back and a box and a belt and a Kilkenny roar: 'There's ball for you!'

I was hurtled savagely into the crowd, stunned, winded,

sick and terrified, and I remember but two things: my head in a girl's lap and her sweet voice saying like an angel, 'I hope the poor little lad isn't dead.'

I closed my eyes. Now was the time to retire from the game in honoured glory. Now, before the pangs of cowardice disgraced me and Mulgannon. I moaned and opened my eyes to see Mulcahy, may God reward him, racing up like a train from the other end of the field to issue to Monsieur Grace a gnarled punch in the heart and two rapid cuts to the forehead that put him securely down on the ground senseless. Scenes ensued wherein the contumelious rejoinder, the raised hand and the taking of the Holy Name frequented.

'Look at what they done to the child,' shouted Mrs Rooney.

'Go on now, dirty butter' and sundry other phrases intimated that the St Fintan's club area principles at play and butter-making left a lot to be desired. Mulcahy and Grace were ordered off the pitch by the referee and left amid the jeers, catcalls and boos of the fickle mob. The home area of the Fintans team was, however, populated by sore hearts and vengeful thoughts for many a long day, as I was to find out.

Throughout the mêlée I remained where I was, with my head in the girl's lap. As soon as I got my breath, I allowed myself to be taken off the pitch by two members of the Sovereign Order of the Knights of Malta. The crowd applauded warmly. The girl with the nice curls told the Knights to be careful of me in case my ribs were broken. I smiled both delicately and gratefully. They were very nice people and after the match both herself and her daddy came around to the Hopes' dressing room and waited until the crowd had gone so that they could enquire after my health. They had the St Fintan's colours up.

That's how it all began. Her name was Noreen Rossiter

and she was studying to be a nurse. This profession in a woman would be very convenient on a farm, particularly at the time of a bad year. But anyhow, she was very pretty, with pearly teeth, a mysterious smile, brown eyes and rosy cheeks. She was taller than I was and she was as well-advantaged a girl in all and several aspects as I ever contemplated. Her daddy had a huge contract for growing sugar beet and in addition to two hundred and forty stall-fed strong cattle he had a strawberry contract and a blackcurrant contract. He lived down a big avenue in a lovely house, which Mrs Mulcahy, stung to jealousy over my position, stated was from George the Third.

The only trouble about these admirable possessions was that he also possessed three sons to fight for the divide. It was fair land. Two rubs of a harrow on ploughed sod would suffice to turn the soil into flour compared with five rubs at home – but with the three in the place, that would earn me no money, especially since two of them had played for the Fintans and carried the scars of that epic. I was not liked and they were jealous of the birds flying over Noreen's head.

One night I said to her, 'Noreen, though my prospects are poor, I am yours forever.' All went well until her daddy found out that I was a nephew of Dick Furlong, who at sixty-eight still went to dances and won old-time waltz competitions. There was a suggestion noised that there might be a history in the Furlong family. The history they were referring to would have been in the realm of insanity. A conspiracy was inaugurated to get rid of me.

That of course was easier planned than executed, for Noreen delighted in my flow of chat while I basked in the truth in her eyes – until the night I reneged on the five. Unhappy strategy!

The card game of Forty-five was an institution of religious

61

significance at Rossiters'. It was solemnly played, and presided over by Mr Rossiter. If one was not a good card-player, one was deemed a mental defective. Mr Rossiter played nearest the fire and kept his soft hat on the back of his head all the time. While considering the cards, he had a pipe clenched between his teeth and at regular intervals cut the red-hot ash in two with tobacco spits. The grunt, 'You deal', followed by the *pwick* of the spit and the *ssheeee* of the saliva boiling on the red-hot logs were features of the night.

I suppose in order to keep the spectre of my uncle Dick away from his mind, Mr Rossiter frequently drew attention to my grandfather, whom he proclaimed: 'One man! One man, I tell you! If you're half as good, you'll do well', and he'd close an eye and nod his head. When I'd play well, he'd say, 'Ah, there was only the one Furlong' and 'God be with your grandfather'. The three sons looked crooked but I began to conclude that I was sprung from noble loins. The weight of all this inherited honour bore deeply on me and made a great impression on my youthful mind, as Adolf Hitler said in his famous book about the world, *Mein Kampf*.

It was a stormy but dry September night which drew us together for what was to be my last game of cards in Rossiters', or anywhere else. The Forty-five game was going well and I had winners all round. Noreen was delighted and smiled at the cunning of my play. Suddenly I started to lose and at the last game of the night I was broke. The last game, they insisted, would be a five-shillings-per-skull pool. There were thirty-five shillings in it altogether, and by some chance my fortune again changed and I ran into a clear lead of forty. The nearest man was thirty. All I wanted was one lousy trick. Noreen's contrary brother dealt. His face perspired hatred above beady eyes peering at me. I was the danger man.

He dealt me nothing but black cards, except for the scarlet

knave of hearts; and hearts were trumps! The dealer's brother led off with the five of trumps. By the rules, I should have played my knave and lost. Suddenly I felt the breeze of Mulgannon blow over me. I saw the mother's face as, inspired, she fought from mud, hunger and adversity through to subsistence. I did not change expression but I hugged the knave to my breast. I knew the mother would have been proud of me. The game and the talk were fast and I played the ten of spades. Then, ecstasies surcease, on the last round the play led into me and I lashed the red knave of hearts down on the table with a crash that rattled the picture of Robert Emmet. 'In the net for the Erin Hopes,' I declared.

Play ceased. A mortuary-chapel silence put its icy hand on the room. In bitter hatred they all turned and looked at me. Noreen brought her handkerchief up to her mouth with a gasp.

'Oh, Nicholas, how could you stoop so low?' And she began to cry.

I thought they wouldn't care. After all, it was only a game. The father rose up from the seat to his full height and removed his quavering hat. He turned his ashen face on me and told me to leave before I brought a curse down on the house.

'I only did it for the laugh,' I remarked, but Noreen emptied a jug of water on top of me and said that she only did that for the laugh. Events took an ugly turn and I decided to terminate my relationship with the house. I withdrew with great dignity and rode like the wind through the village of Killinick amid a shower of stones and sods from her brothers and ribald jeers from the rustics. It will be a long time before I'm caught in that vicinity again.

6

THE GIRL FROM RATHGAW

I now intend to deal with a reverse which had a great effect on the formation of my character.

It happened in the summer of 1949, when a Gaelic-football tournament for Midasian gold trophies was nearing its climax. The trophies were presented by a Wexford man, home rich from America, to commemorate the men who fought in the rebellion of 1798. The tournament started in 1948 on the one-hundred-and-fiftieth anniversary of the rising. As happy fate would have it, the two teams to reach the final were Wexford, the county which put manners on the empire, and Meath, where the last stands in Leinster were taken.

There was a fever of excitement in the town. Mulcahy was blue in the face with anticipation, for he was a potential star himself. Transport was the problem, but it was slapped up to me before the final in Croke Park, Dublin, that the sow's time was up to farrow that very Sunday. Arrangements would have to be made, for fear the sow would lie on the bonhams as soon as they were farrowed. Our sow was ignorant and hostile as well. The last time she farrowed I had to stand behind a wall and take the bons from under her with a four-tagged fork and she snapping and frothing. It took her eight hours to have six bons and she lay on two.

If I had been listened to, she would by this time have been an eaten sausage. But no. There were those in authority who knew better than Nicholas, those who had been through the mill, those who had borne the burden of the day and the heats. So she snarled her way to a further pregnancy with the gentleman pig owned by Mr Mulcahy. Mr Mulcahy always referred in my presence to bulls and boars as 'the gentleman'. Mr Mulcahy was very proper in the presence of youth.

I began to consider more noble places to be that Sunday than minding the farrowing sow with my life in my hands. Was I to stay at home while a further page of glory was to be inscribed upon Wexford's storied annals? I began a campaign to get off for the day, and not alone that, but to get the van as well. I informed the mother that remarks were passed in a certain house that young Mr Mulcahy seemed to be able to transport the whole of Mulgannon around Ireland without thanks or return.

The next day the mother remarked that it would not be right to expect Mr Mulcahy to bring me everywhere; there would be certain parties in the locality only too pleased to pass comment on it behind people's backs. I was to take the van and bring young Mr Mulcahy, whom she trusted to look after me, and, if I wished, Nellie MacDonagh's youngest son, who looked as if he could do with something else besides minced meat for the dinner. 'But be coming across Wexford Bridge on the stroke of eleven o'clock in Rowe Street chapel, or I'll break your blasted neck,' the mother said.

The mother gave me three pound notes before we set out. It was a lot of money in those days, not faulting the woman. We set off, Mulcahy, MacDonagh and I, down the hill of Mulgannon as the sun danced on the lough of Wexford which had seen the Celtic and Danish hordes, the Norman and Cromwellian, the blood of martyrs and spongers, of yeomen, rebels and saints and the thousand tomato-flecked vomits of the drunkard. Mrs MacDonagh shook holy water over the van as we left. I remarked on the piety of the ancient Irish. Mulcahy said it was in case the van fell apart. Mulcahy could be very spiteful.

We had right gas on the way up. Sometimes when we'd pass a nice girl on a bike, MacDonagh would lower the window and shout, 'Eh, miss, how is your mother for spuds?' or 'Hello girls, here's fellas!' and 'Eh, hon, would you do the bold thing?' On one occasion we passed a whole string of girls cycling along the Glen of the Downs, all very nice with short pants and coloured jumpers. MacDonagh pulled his trousers way up over his knees, displaying spindly, hairy legs. He thrust these out the window and started to wag them up and down and scream, 'Squeals of maiden anguish, *wheeeeee!*'

The girls nearly fell off the bikes with the laughing and they all waved like mad. It was a pity we had to get to the match. Just outside Bray, we pulled up and sat down on the footpath. We had flasks of tea and soup, corned beef and ham sandwiches, apple cake, currant bread and scones. MacDonagh had a pint bottle of stout, which he was not too bashful to drink in public. Mulcahy remarked that some people regarded their Confirmation pledge very lightly. This did not affect MacDonagh, who bet one shilling that he could spit farther than anyone past the white line in the middle of the road, the best of three spits to be the winner. This intrigued Mulcahy, and I fancied my chances too because out in the land you get a lot of practice, especially at dirty jobs or windy days.

It was my turn to spit. I gave a good hawk and lobbed a breadcrumb spit well over the line, when by us drove Mulcahy's sister with her boyfriend, the dispensary doctor. He was laughing as he drove by but she pretended not to see us, although we raised enough of a row to be heard in an aeroplane. She appeared very cross but I put no pass on that for, living with a woman, I was well used to the moods and notions that women take. MacDonagh won the long-spit competition and was well contented when he received our two shillings, which he later expended on another pint of stout.

When we got to Croke Park, the Wexford team were marching around the field in the parade, led by the Artane boys' band, playing 'Kelly from Killanne'. There they were, under the eyes of cheering thousands and the pageantry of the greatest stadium in Ireland, fellows we knew well to see in the streets – Willie Goodison, Seanie Sinnott, Wilkie Thorpe, Jim Coady, Spider Kelly of Ballymitty and the one man, known all over Ireland from photographs and repute, Peter MacDermot of Royal Meath, with glistening, smooth black hair, sallow Maori appearance and lithe, slippery eyes darting with intelligence. The parade was over, the national anthem chanted with feeling, the white ball tossed in and the game was on.

What a game! It was as if the thirty players no longer commanded their limbs or deeds. It was as if Almighty God with celestial fingers throbbed and dictated the trend of play as if He were playing an organ or conducting an orchestra for the delight and astonishment of mortal man. A fantastic incident, save, heroism, greyhound movement, pinpoint precision, ground-devouring clearance, one after the other for the entire match kept the crowd in a continual roar that never stopped until our hearts stopped; for in the closing minutes a slight slip, a miscalculation on one end of the field caused a score in the other. Victory was turned to defeat. Wexford had lost.

We mooched down O'Connell Street with sick stomachs. We got our tea in a restaurant on Burgh Quay which gave four-course lunches for two and six. I was that revolted about the match that I swore I wouldn't go home.

'What'll we do then?' asked MacDonagh in a funeral voice.

'We'll go to a dance, that's what we'll do,' I said.

'The very thing,' decided Mulcahy.

A West Indian singer named Jon Clarke was all the rage in Dublin and his worshippers went to hear him spread his chalky palms, open his eyes and sway his hips at the Crystal Ballroom. Immediately the swing-door opened it was like walking into heaven. There was a sudden bass blast of an orchestra playing a slow waltz. Girls, dressed in shimmering frocks, swayed and danced cheek-to-cheek under a revolving crystal ball. On all the walls there were huge mirrors, so that the place looked like Versailles by Direaux, hanging up in the Mulcahys' best room. For one horrifying second I was chilled to the liver when I thought of Mulgannon and the wicked sow farrowing. I didn't want to pretend to either of the other two nyuks that I was impressed with the surroundings. So I remarked that I didn't come here to scratch for spuds. I busied myself immediately on the chase.

I happened to be beautifully dressed, so that it wouldn't occur to any Dublin girl that I was from the country. You can imagine my surprise when the first girl I asked up to dance said, looking me straight in the eye, 'You're from the country yourself, aren't you? Are you up for the match?'

'You're very quick,' said I, and one word borrowed another so successfully that after my second dance with her, I asked her up to the balcony for lemonade. The two revolutionaries I had with me nearly got sick with jealousy.

The mother instructed me about occasions like this. 'Never humble yourself in company, Nicholas,' she said. 'When you are asked outright, always add a few acres to what you've got. No one will know any better at the time and there'll be enough to drag you down to their own level in the heel of the hunt.'

She was a very refined girl named Veronica Russell, from Rathgaw, an important district of Dublin. She told me that she was engaged in commerce.

'I suppose you're a farmer,' she said. 'Have you much land?'

'Ah, not much, Veronica,' said I. 'About two hundred and forty-nine acres or thereabouts.'

I brought her home to Rathgaw that night, but you know how much business I could transact with the other two open-mouthed gawks in the back with their ears cocked and they passing remarks.

She was gorgeous. I could not take my eyes off her when she walked before me. She used to swing a little but not much and occasionally she'd extend her long fingers and softly put a wisp of brown hair back into place. She had a red frock, a belt tight around a revolving waist, a string of pearls and white shiny shoes. She smelled like the furze flower in bloom. But what a dancer! In a South American dance she didn't seem to move at all but swayed, raised my hand and danced in under it. When my mind glanced home and I thought of the women who move like potato sacks, I nearly went mad. How could I just bugger off that night away from her? I made a date for lunch with her the very next day. Yes, Monday. I would not go home for love or money.

I parked the van in Harcourt Street, opened up a bag of straw and slept there until morning. In the middle of the night MacDonagh gave a hollow 'Ooooowahhhyok' and vomited his lights out onto the street from the back of the van. 'Serves him feckin' well right,' I allowed. Savaging a whiskey was the last I saw of him in the Crystal. I put the two nuisances on the first train to Wexford after borrowing

69

four pound notes from Mulcahy. The instruction I gave them was to say that the van dynamo was cracked and that I was having it repaired.

My heart was bursting in the hot sun until twelve o'clock. I met her outside the park gates in Stephen's Green. She knew a nice place for a meal by the name of Jammets – as a matter of fact, the owners were relatives of her own. It was a grand place, with men in dicky bows and swallow tails there to wait hand and foot. We were given the menu while we waited. A man asked us if we wanted a drink. I wasn't bothered, but I thought that perhaps Miss Russell might like one. But Veronica said very civilly that it was rather early and she'd rather not. There were large glass tanks in the room with all sorts of fish, big and small, swimming around. Veronica told me that, if I preferred the fish course, the waiter would select the fish of my choice in the tank, catch it and cook it. But I wasn't on for fish. I had a pain in the arse at home looking at herrings and whiting.

I must tell you about the menu book. It was large and stiff, very unusual, and there was a coloured drawing of a bird's feather on the cover, almost like a cock pheasant's. Inside, however, it was naturally full of writing and prices, but there wasn't one scrap of English language in the whole issue. I brought it home with me. The only snip of English that was on it was '10 per cent in lieu of gratuities' and a bit about car-parking facilities.

Veronica knew what it was all about. She could speak French. She had '*huitres de Galway*' herself but ordered some class of soup for me (to be exact, it was '*soupe à l'oignon gratinée*'). She ordered a thing called '*faisan roti sur canapé*' for herself. I didn't want to display my ignorance and I spotted one word I understood. I also had a shot at pronouncing it myself – '*Le steak au poivre blanc flambé au vieux cognac.*'

The butler with the notebook got it right anyhow, although I thought later that he was a bit dilatory about attending to his duties.

The grub was all right. I made only two simple mistakes. I broke up the bread scones into the soup and I spilled a jug of water. I apprehended that things took a turn for the worse after that. Veronica wasn't half the gas she was the previous night. I had to go into the kitchen after the waiter for the tea. He was so long out there that I thought he'd gone down to a boat on the Liffey to get it. When I brought it back, the tea leaves were stuck and Veronica said, 'You ought to blow down the spout.'

It was a good idea so I did that and my lips nearly stuck to the silver. It was red hot and I was going to lash it out through the window when she stood straight up, grabbed her handbag and vanished out the door. Her lovely skirt swinging in the sunshine was the last I saw of her forever. Life is curious. I was that alarmed and annoyed, I rushed out after her without paying or looking for the bill.

Then to have to face back to Mulgannon. All the way down the road I was haunted by a vision of the mother's chopping gob and she like a briar – that is, if she was still there and not eaten alive by the sow. But thanks be to God, things took a turn for the better. I drew up inside the gate, where the first thing she hit me with was where I got the money to fix the repairman. She was looking at me like a wasp with one eye shut.

'Mrs Mulcahy gave the young lad a lot of money, mother,' I said, 'and he gave me a loan of four pounds.'

That softened the cough on her. In order that the matter of the loan would not be slapped up to her or me in the future, she gave me four green notes to pay back Mulcahy that very day. I gave Mulcahy and MacDonagh one pound each to keep their mouths shut and I kept two pounds' expenses for myself.

The sow had farrowed in the middle of the Sunday night without anyone going next, near or by her. She had fourteen of the finest bons you ever laid eyes on. There wasn't a mark or scratch on any of them and the sow herself was as contented as a flea on a sheepdog. The mother wanted to know when I was going to leave the place again, because she noticed that there was an absence of agitation.

I got over Veronica. Of course, I went up in the estimation of Mulcahy and MacDonagh because they had no way of knowing what had transpired. As the mother always maintained, 'Once down, Nicholas, never lost a race.' When all is said and done, the mother had the head bolted on.

7

THE SERGEANT'S DAUGHTER

The subject of this chapter is the sergeant's daughter. I have written on a scrap of paper all the headings as they happened in order of time, so that I will forget nothing. Yet even at that, it may be thought that a lot of it is invention. The only thing I can say is that it can all be checked in Wexford town and details can be found in the files of the *Free Press*.

There arrived in Wexford town a new sergeant of the guards, or Garda Síochána, as the police are known. This man's name was Sergeant Joseph Busher. He was the prescribed height and had a cross, windswept face which never smiled. His reputation came before him. He was the strictest guard in Ireland and upheld every letter of the law with such fanaticism that he had been transferred four times on appeals from the local TD. He had an advanced antipathy to drink of an alcoholic nature.

The mother said that all policemen had the upper hand and if they told you your hat was on the wrong way, the proper retort was 'Yes, sir, that's right.' She said that the old Royal Irish Constabulary – before they were shot down like pigeons – and the guards were all one sack, one sample. The mother knew who was scruff and who was quality. I observed myself that when she read the papers to me reporting the deaths or marriages of those she considered quality, she read out the notices with a grand accent. I asked her who the gentry were anyway.

'That's a question, Nicholas, that's easier asked than answered,' the mother replied. 'Rather is it easier to say those who are not gentry than those who are. Shopkeepers aren't gentry and neither are dentists. I could answer you about bank clerks if I knew their seed, breed and generation. To be really gentry, you have, of course, to own land or be a gynaecologist or a judge or a colonel in the British army or a Protestant who is rotten with money. But of course,' and here she smiled sweetly in reflection and stole me a sidelong glance, 'there's no gentry left in the country now, Nicholas.'

I wasn't going to waste my time arguing with a mad woman. Privately I could not accept that a guard could be as strict as this man. My tune was soon changed, for I witnessed an event which astounded me. It took place at the second Wexford Opera Festival of Music and the Arts. It put a great respect and fear of police into my mind.

The Wexford Opera Festival of that time and to this day had and has operatic offerings of a world standard. The continued success of this festival is indicative of the surviving spirit of Wexford, the spirit which rose up against oppressor and planter, cut-throat and Dane, begrudger and thwarter, empire and Antichrist from the mist of prehistory to the present day.

The chief spur of the Wexford Festival was an anaesthetist named Dr Thomas J. Walsh, a member of a distinguished Wexford family. During the festival, the town is thronged with visitors. They range from musicians, opera singers, actors, composers, writers, conductors and music lovers (genuine and mock) to parasites and loafers from all over the world.

Mulcahy was a genuine music lover and he played the piano by ear. His parents held musical evenings in their house. He went to all the things in the festival with his mother, older brothers or his sister. He gave us all the rots, talking about everything he'd seen, and was able to make statements with great authority such as, 'I find that Monto-vecchi has greater fluency of expression than Tosstrova.' Neither MacDonagh nor I had a notion what he was talking about but we were afraid to show the remotest symptom of levity in case the big shagger would kick the beans out of the two of us. MacDonagh commented that he would carry with him to the grave the sorrow that he had not heard those excellent gentlemen sing. I passed the remark that I'd sing well too if I had as much beer and women as they had. Mulcahy threw a look of contempt on me. However, he paused for several minutes and then said that the Italian opera singers sang every night in the back bar of White's Hotel around eleven.

We made arrangements to consummate our awakened artistic appetite. We wanted to drink a draught of the frenzy, excitement and spectacle of the festival, which lived like an epidemic for two exhausting weeks. But it cost an awful lot of money, and, what's more, you had to have a black dress suit and dicky bow. Those two hurdles and the obstacle of parental permission were overcome in miraculous fashion. Mulcahy had a dress suit of his own. A loan of his bothers' suits for MacDonagh and me was negotiated. Three tickets for a special concert by Rampoli, who was to play the fiddle in the Capitol Cinema on Saturday night, were donated by Mrs Mulcahy.

It was Mrs Mulcahy who asked the mother to let me off, pointing out that it would be good for the boy's training. 'A perception of what is best in music stands one always in good stead,' Mrs Mulcahy said. The mother was quick to point out that Nicholas of course had music in his blood.

His granduncle Joseph, of Land League fame, had won first prize at the New Ross Feis senior lament for fiddles in 1912. The mother also showed Mrs Mulcahy his memorial card.

We had to promise to be home before half twelve that night and that we would not break our Confirmation pledges, a condition that MacDonagh agreed to. We walked down the Mulgannon road in the Mulcahys' lovely dress suits with light hearts. The only untoward event occurred at the outskirts of the town, near the junction of Michael Street and Barrack Street. Moses Flaherty, a member of the labouring classes, walked out of Curtis's provision shop and saw the three of us. He kept his eye on me and seemed to be in a state of paralysis, for as we passed together he pressed himself up against the wall, removed his cap and blessed himself. He also called out the proprietor, Mr Thomas Curtis, and a customer to witness what he had seen. I was waiting for some remark befitting his station, such as 'Go on now, feck the horsehair' or some other rustic address, but he must have been struck dumb.

Charlie Hipwell, who looked at me as if I had leprosy, showed us to our seats amid a most impressive array of furs, pelts, earrings and perfume. Jealousy, you see. I wouldn't be fit to be in that company, oh no. The mother told me that I could hold my head up high before any of the Hipwells. They were the scrapings of hell who landed with Cromwell and had the presence of mind to conform to the true Church when the thing got too hot.

Each of the tickets cost one pound one shilling. The programme cost seven and six. All this was generously donated by Mrs Mulcahy of Mulgannon House. However, I was grey at the return for this expense. Without putting a tooth on it, Mr Rampoli wouldn't be fit to resin a string for Charlie Fitzgerald, who when sober could wring tears from a steel helmet with 'The Rocks of Bawn' or 'The Croppy Boy'. I was stuck between a friar who hummed in Italian and Mulcahy, who smiled knowledgeably. He nodded his head from side to side to indicate that he knew each phrase and subtlety. MacDonagh sat hunched in his seat sideways, with his ear cocked, as it were, to the stage. It was plain from where I was that his attentions were on a lady who, although older than us, was not completely clothed, in that a soft portion of her upper person was visible, to the detriment of purity.

None of the tunes which Mr Rampoli played had names on them. For example, there was this legend on the programme: 'Sonata in D Major Op. 12 No. 1' by the famous German, Beethoven. And again 'Partita No. 2 in D Minor' by Bach. Wouldn't you think he'd have the presence of mind to play a tune from the country that was forking out the cash?

We got down to White's Hotel at a quarter past ten with Mulcahy in charge. 'The two of you remain close to my back,' he said. He put his huge bulk into what appeared to be a mass of aristocracy and native Irish, all with glasses in their hands or cigars or cigarettes in holders, talking loudly and with much mirth.

The front hall was jammed, and flustered waiters struggled with trays of glasses. Mulcahy bid a lofty 'goodnight' to several people and occasionally looked back to see if we were coming. We eventually got into the large lounge bar, which was bedded with a red carpet and populated by smoke-engulfed intellectuals.

'Here is where they sing,' Mulcahy announced, and asked very importantly what we wished to drink. MacDonagh said he'd prefer a gin and tonic for a start to kill the beetles. I declared for orange squash. Mulcahy said, 'Certainly. Keep your eyes open for seats. If anyone gets up, claim them at once.'

He came back to us after surely ten minutes with a fruit juice for himself, a squash for me and the gin and tonic for MacDonagh, who drained his glass in two seconds and said that there was a taste of more off it. He disappeared and returned shortly with the same again. Mulcahy announced the arrival of Ponti and Kallamangas, the tenor and bass stars of the opera. There was a roar of applause as the two yellow-faced, black-haired gentlemen entered.

Without waiting to be asked at all, the huge Kallamangas laughed, waved and broke into a lively Italian song. With effortless ease, he broadsided enough power to shred the bar mirror. I never heard the like of it in my life. A roar of appreciation and then a full tumbler of brandy was put into his mighty hand. He deferred to his colleague Ponti, who by this time was nursing a similar beverage as well as a girl of unchaste display. He put his arm around her and sang with great verve and humour a song I've never forgotten called 'Questa o Quella'. I bought a record of it the next week.

MacDonagh informed me that it was damn well near time I bought a round and that his was a pint of porter. He intimated that I had been nursing the money and fondling my person. I returned with his pint and an orange squash for Mulcahy. I had enough already in my glass to last. It was now half past eleven. All bars have to shut at eleven sharp but an extension was given for festival weeks.

I arrive now at a most important part of the night. Mulcahy, MacDonagh and I were centrally situated and in command of three seats opposite the bar entrance. Mulcahy spent his time inhaling the atmosphere of enlightened discourse. MacDonagh was involved with a gentleman who in swarthy appearance resembled one of the three wise men in the Bride Street chapel crib. They had begun to esteem one another so well that they commenced to buy one another drinks, to our exclusion.

Opposite us, sitting down, almost hidden behind a pint glass of frothy Guinness was Mr Donagh Cunningham, who was district justice of all County Wexford. The mother told me he was up against the clergy and couldn't have luck. Be that as it may, I was wishing I had a share of whatever it was he was having. He was pontificating on the poetry of an ignorant Monaghan man and made his points with both arms outstretched over the porter as if offering an oblation. All the fingers of his hands were extended and he twisted them to right and left in the fervour of his observations. Once a drunkard came over to him and offered to buy him a jar and all of his mates. This generous imposition didn't register for ten seconds but when it did Mr Cunningham summoned up the words in Adam's-apple gulps and addressed the hopeful donor thus: 'For the sake of Him who died upon rood, *go eh-way!*' The rebuffed and insulted citizen went away declaring that that was the crowd ruling the country today, the leavings of the Black and Tans.

The babble, the backslapping and solos went on amidst cheer and fellowship. Then, most abruptly, an electrifying apparition intruded. The door of the lounge bar was pushed brutally open. There appeared before the gaze of all a spectacle both incongruous and frightening. As if cut off by a mighty lever, conversation stopped instantly. Framed, frozen and belligerent in the door was a huge ulcerated-faced Sergeant of the Garda Siochána of Éireann in full uniform, giving every indication that he had discovered an orgy of carnal violence.

Mr White, the proprietor of the hotel, was the first to recover.

'Good evening, Sergeant Busher, can I help you?'

'Are you aware, sir, that closing time was eleven o'clock?' the sergeant asked.

'I'm afraid there's some mistake, sergeant,' Mr White said. 'There is an extension until three AM throughout the festival.'

'There is indeed a mistake, sir,' the sergeant said. 'The extension applies every night except Saturday night.'

Mr White's face altered considerably for the worse. The sergeant called to the doorway, 'Guard!'

Enter Mick Wynn, a decent senior guard who had been in Wexford all his life and never said boo to a blackguard. He came in on shamefaced tiptoe as if he was paying tribute to a corpse. He had a notebook in his hand.

'What's your name, sir?' the sergeant asked the first gentleman to his right hand.

'Giovanni Kallamangas, Milano,' the giant smiled.

'Are you stopping in this hotel, sir?'

'Si.'

He passed on. 'What's your name, sir?'

'Denis Philip Crosby.'

'Are you stopping in this hotel, sir?'

'No, I'm from the Faythe, Wexford.'

'Take that man's name, Guard. What's your name, sir?'

'Donagh James Cunningham, district justice in this area; I'm not stopping here, Guard. I am stopping in the Talbot Hotel, and you should know me, if I may say so.'

To the great astonishment of the beholders, this dispatch of words might just as profitably have been delivered to the Redmond Monument.

'Yes sir, I do, but I am compelled to undertake the regulated formalities. Take his name, Guard. And what is your name, sir?'

'John Brendan Hearne, Assistant Commissioner of the

Garda Síochána, Phoenix Park, Dublin, at the moment residing in the Talbot Hotel.'

'Take that gentleman's name also, Guard.'

He proceeded down the line.

'Your name, sir?'

'Marcellino Ponti, Napoli – White's Hotella, Wexforda.'

'Your name, sir?'

A huge, bearded gentleman got up. He was like Our Lord. I recognised him as a rope-maker from New Ross. However, with great presence of mind he announced a name out loud.

'Andria O Minnicoia, O Rossa; *si.*'

'Disregard the Italians, Guard. Your name, sir?'

'Alphonsus Joseph Mulcahy, Mulgannon House, Wexford.' Mulcahy was shitting himself with the fright. He was not alone in this. So was I.

'Take his name.'

'How old are you?'

'I'm gone twenty-one,' I protectively volunteered, 'and my name is Nicholas Joseph Patrick Furlong of Mulgannon, Wexford.'

'Take his name.'

MacDonagh, fortified and objective about the matter, informed the sergeant that he was Leslie de Burca, second violin on the Radio Éireann Orchestra, residing in White's Hotel. The sergeant passed on without a second glance and as soon as he did, MacDonagh hooked it out the door, not to be seen for ten days.

There were black looks abroad in the night, none more black than the looks which crossed the faces of the arbiters of justice in the land, District Justice Cunningham and Assistant Commissioner Hearne. There was a Jesuit from Clongowes Wood College caught and an intellectual parish priest from the archdiocese of Dublin among forty-seven other lay members of the several Churches suffering.

I may say here now that there wasn't another word about it. No case was brought. Not that the mother nor I would have minded, for I would be in the paper in good company, namely the quality of Ireland and not the dregs.

That was the first time I laid eyes on Sergeant Busher, a bitter-hearted hoor's melt if ever I laid eyes on one. I vowed to keep far away from him, because he put the fear of God in my windpipe.

Four weeks later I attended a pioneer reunion with Mulcahy in the St John of God School. A pioneer is a term I should have explained. It refers to a group of people who eschew all intoxicating liquor for the greater glory of God and the honour of Ireland.

The pioneer social cost only two shillings and for that small sum there was a band, a dance, a sit-down supper of tea, sandwiches, cakes and biscuits and a lot of lovely girls who were also pioneers. Mulcahy was a strict total abstainer with strong views on drink. It took a whole night of arguing and persuasion from me to alter his intention to maim MacDonagh when he first discovered he had broken his pledge. Mulcahy was secretary of the young pioneers and he made me join too.

The pioneer reunion was my first function in the movement. We stood around the hall inspecting all the girls. Mulcahy of course was busy seeing that everything was all right. The band was quite reasonable for the occasion. In the dancing I was taken by a winsome girl. She had fair wavy hair, slightly freckled skin, a strong handsome face which smiled rarely but when it did it opened like a buttercup. She had a dark green dress with buttons down the front and a belt of the same material. She had light-brown silk stockings with a seam down the back of them, which occasioned a challenge to the virtue of chastity. There were other lovely girls there too, but I couldn't take my eyes off her, for while I knew everyone else by sight at least, she was a total stranger.

Mulcahy must have seen my mouth open. He came around by the back of the other fellows standing there like dummies, tapped me on the shoulder and indicated with his head that he wanted to see me. I withdrew in annoyance from the front ranks and asked him if it was a pain that was on him.

'Do you know who the bird is in the green dress?' he asked.

'No, I don't. Who is she?'

'She is none other,' said Mulcahy, 'than the daughter of that busy officer of the police force, Sergeant Joseph Busher.'

'Sweet Sacred Heart of Jesus, preserve us all here this night,' I said in prayer. I did not know it at the time but that terrifying spectre was shortly to be of intimate yet destructive significance both to me and to Katherine Aquinas Furlong, widow. I had made arrangements to meet his daughter Marie at the Redmond Monument the following Wednesday night.

*

The mother threw down the spoon from her mouth.

'The world, the world, jealousies and begrudgers,' she exclaimed. This at half six in the morning and the moon still shining.

'Woman, don't be taking the heart out of me at this hour of the morning. Lash into your porridge there; to hell out of that with your "The world, the world, jealousies and be-grudgers" at half six in the middle of the night – you give me the rots.'

'Oh,' says she, 'I was thinking of poor Father and it all came back before my mind, how he was thwarted at every step. I'm warning you now, Nicholas, the only true friend a boy has in this world is his own mother.'

I knew well what all this was about. This was for my benefit because the mother was told by Nellie MacDonagh that the new sergeant's daughter was very taken with Nicholas. 'A brillent girl, all belonging to her brillent, first in Irish and biological chemistry in St Louis, Bunclody and then the Leaving Certificate, ninety-eight marks in each subject out of a hundred. Bursting with brains, the whole lot of them, brillent.' Marie Busher, the wicked sergeant's daughter, liked my style and told me I had a good sense of humour and a nice voice. She also told me that if I grew a bit I would be suited to the guards.

I always called her 'Freckles' after that and she didn't mind a bit. She was very refined and said it was her ambition to marry a farmer. For all I knew that could have been me because the mother always swore that I'd fall in for a lot. I'd have the home place and the uncle's place and his money as well, provided he didn't give it to some slattern. I always made sure to give the impression that there was more than a galvanised shed at my back. I begged Marie to let me take her to the annual Garda dance in the Golf Hotel, Rosslare.

I didn't encourage the company of Mulcahy or Mac-Donagh, although I noted their presence in the dance hall as soon as I crunched up the gravel to the entrance with Marie. Mr MacDonagh senior was a great friend of the guards and always bought two tickets for every ball but never went himself. That, I suppose, is how the other two spies got in. Anyhow, I told them on the way in that I didn't want any torment from any of them for the rest of the night. Mac-Donagh wanted to know if Marie would be on for the queer thing. I would have given him a clatter in the snot for himself there and then, only for Mulcahy.

It was a rattling good night, with Kevin O'Mahoney's band and lashings of spot prizes and women of all ages and sizes. Thank God I didn't have the torment of wearing myself out searching for talent when I was after paying for it at the entrance. Marie looked only divine with an off-the-forehead perm, real gold earrings and an aquamarine frock with white collar and short sleeves. She wore a bronze bangle with a Celtic motif, giving an indication of her scholarship. There wasn't a woman in the hall fit to hand her a ruled jotter. I wore a dark-blue bum-freezer coat myself with a Young Farmers' club badge in the buttonhole.

Marie asked me to meet her daddy. I'd have sooner gone up the gallows but I went up to him anyhow. He was deep in conversation with two other large gentlemen but when Marie introduced me he sized me up and forced a teeth strip from himself. He made some ha-ha remark like 'Mind you keep off the grass, now.'

There was a nice young guard doing MC although he was sucking up to the sergeant all the time. He noted Marie with me so he sidled up and asked me to oblige the company by rendering a song. Marie pressed my hand and smiled encouragement. I decided to sing a respectable song so I went up on the stand and sang the mother's favourite 'I Dreamt that I Dwelt'. There was a great response to it and many shouts of 'More' and 'One voice'. In fairness I must say that MacDonagh and Mulcahy, who divided to different sectors of the hall, gave a great hand with the cheers.

I carried on with the mother's second favourite, 'The Heart Bowed Down with Weal and Woe'. This also had a very good reception and I was persuaded to contribute another song. It was 'Asleep in the Deep', which the uncle taught me years ago for Christmas.

Marie's father said that I had a nice voice if it had been

trained in my youth. I got on well with the young guard although I didn't have the satisfaction of his company for very long. The week after the dance he was transferred to Achill, an island off the coast of Mayo. I was informed later that Sergeant Busher was in a froth, because his daughter's escort's voice had been overexploited. It greatly increased my apprehension of that gentleman.

*

The mother took a notion to buy a bike after receiving a bill for petrol and repairs to the van. A bike! And the only part of her body that was fit to work was her head. She got a second-hand bike, a Pierce, with double-barrelled crossbars and a big bell. She insisted that I teach her how to ride it.

'Right,' I said, 'I'll teach you in one easy lesson.'

I knew myself that there was only one way to learn and that was to take off down the hill. I brought her up to the crown of the hill of Mulgannon. I showed her how to start, travel and stop. There wasn't any danger, for the slope was light and there were acres of ferns and bushes on the side of the road. It was a mile further down the road where the hill descended into Wexford town that the slope was severe. I waited until the coast was clear and obtained confirmation that her intent of purpose had not waned. She had her glasses strapped on with elastic and wore wellington boots to protect her shins. I saw her mounted safely in the saddle and said, 'Now, Mother, it's either sink or swim: off you go,' and I pushed her off.

She took off erect and got up speed heading for Wexford town. That was all right until I saw her heading straight for the big hill, grimly holding on to her bike, with her widow's folds flapping in the wind behind her. Panic seized me. I started to run, shouting 'Brake! Brake!' But she entered the steep Mulgannon hill splitting in fright colonies of hens, cats and mongrels. The bell kept ringing like a fire engine.

At the bottom of the long hill there was an assortment of horse-drawn caravans and two temporary tents on the side of the road outside Cromwell's Fort, the residence of the wealthy shipowner and merchant prince, James J. Stafford. That morning I had noted the presence at the site of five piebald ponies, seven thin greyhounds, three caravans and about twenty of our travelling brothers and sisters. The mother was now on their horizon. I arrived at the top of the steep slope with my heart in my mouth. I saw her shave by four citizens of the travelling culture and then rocket straight up the angled steps of a caravan with a crash and glass-shattering thud that brought everyone in the camp out screaming and with ashplants drawn. The caravan lurched forward, hit the next caravan with a thud, two piebalds bolted into Wexford and there were shouts in which recourse was had to the Holy Name.

A cruising squad car drew up. 'What's all this about?' Sergeant Busher asked.

I watched with the liver horrified out of me from the back of Stafford's wall. The mother came out of the caravan shaking herself. She might have been overcome by concussion but apart from that she was not one hair the worse. Sergeant Busher would not have known the mother. I made it my business not to let them meet but he often enquired for her health. He considered that the female person in front of him was a member of the travelling society engaging in internecine strife.

'Who are you, a scaldy-faced turnip from the bogs of Kerry, to ask me, Katherine Aquinas Furlong, who I am?' the mother said. 'The likes of you,' she said, 'should only be let loose amongst decent people on a judge's licence. I was born and reared on my own land, thanks be to God, and no poteen sponge from the swamps of Munster is going to tell me my business.'

'Proceed, Guard, to this amazon's holding,' Sergeant Busher said to his companion, 'and investigate the obnoxious weeds situation.'

*

The courtroom in Wexford County Hall is designed to put respect for Mother Ireland on the delinquent, humility on the litigant and brazenness on the advocates who revel in their theatrics. The mother and I were put alongside Bangers Ryan, who was up for loitering with intent. It was not a position of social elevation, and to give her her due, the mother was used to better days. But she dressed like a respectable widow of farming ancestry in solemn black, a subdued hat and a brooch. To show coolness to the uniformed hordes from Kerry, Donegal and Connemara who peered across the courtroom in menacing demeanour, she engaged in lively conversation with the malefactor, Bangers Ryan. Mr Ryan had an inexhaustible fund of legal knowledge.

The judge's box, as well as the witness box, was high up in the sky. At the back of the judge's box was emblazoned in blue and gold the harp of Ireland, to indicate that, though all would get a fair crack of the whip, the butt of it would be gripped in the fair hand of Kathleen Ní Hualacháin. There was a rake of loafers and corner boys in the public gallery as there was a varied and interesting card to be run off. In addition to the mother's case, there were four civil bills, an eviction, a malicious damage, two dangerous-drivings, a loitering-with-intent, twenty-four gentlemen-caught-in-licensed-premises-after-hours, fourteen offences-against-the-traffic-act and one preliminary-carnal-knowledge.

The district justice appeared. All rose. The mother's eye followed him up with head bent on shoulder. Justice Donagh James Cunningham was clad in black robes and white wig. He sat down on the bench with a sour expression on his face and looked all around him to see if the windows were closed against the draught. The justice said he would deal with the civil bills and minor cases first and the more serious cases later, so the mother's case wasn't called until half past two in the afternoon. She decided, in view of a belief that the judge had a grudge against Catholic clergy, it might be better if she got a Protestant to defend her. She put her fate into the heretical hands of Mr E. G. Hume, a well-known sportsman and wit whose forefathers had taken both shilling and soup.

The interests of the travelling fraternity were protected by the greatest criminal lawyer in Ireland, Mr J. F. I. Connors, a man who dispatched his commissions with oratory and discretion. The superintendent of the guards prosecuted on behalf of Ireland and the chief witness was Sergeant Joseph Busher. He mounted the witness box, removed his cap, took the oath and endeavoured to have sentence of death passed on the mother.

Jerry Lacey, the representative of the travelling persuasion, was well schooled. He had the whole story like a song. When he described the descent of the mother upon the tribe he turned right around to the judge and said, 'Begor, sir, at one time I thought she'd take off and fly.' The judge scribbled in his book, glancing from one page to the other. I thought it was that one sentence rather than calling the sergeant a scaldy-faced guttersnipe that put the last nail in the mother's coffin.

I wasn't given much trouble at all and it was Justice Cunningham himself who asked me questions, almost paternally. He asked me what age my mother was and I replied, 'A hardy sixty-nine.' So she was hardy. She'd put her hand into a nest of rats and knock their brains out on a dashed wall if the need arose.

'Was your mother a frequent cyclist?'

I had to tell the man that it was her first lesson. He stopped, looked at me and behaved in peculiar fashion, as if trying to swallow his Adam's apple, and moved his head up and down like a duck gargling water.

Mr Foster Lennon, the surveyor, produced a map and explained the extent of the gradient on the hill of Mulgannon. This intelligence imparted with calm narrative had a great impression on the district justice. The mother was called.

The mother became all granny and sighs and smiles at the justice when she got into the box to answer her nine charges. (Speeding in a manner etc.; defective front brakes; no reflector; in charge of a bicycle while unfit by reason of a physical defect; causing damage to two caravans, personal effects and a suit, the property of one Isaac Cash, to the extent of twenty-one pounds eighteen shillings and nine pence; obstructing the gardaí in the execution of their duty; abusive language to an officer of the gardaí; five acres' infestation of obnoxious weeds.)

The mother simpered in half-genteel fashion under her hat and bun with steel-rimmed glasses glinting. 'Ah, Mr Cunningham, sir, you know the way it would be now, you've a mother yourself.'

She might as well have tried to soft-soap a provoked Alsatian. When all the evidence was heard, the assembled citizens awaited the judge's verdict. He removed his glasses and wiped them slowly with his handkerchief. He looked far off, as if gazing at a distant mountain over the slopes of which he himself had been dragged by savages.

'I have served on the bench in County Wexford since 1945 and prior to that in Roscommon and Leitrim. I have never heard the like before. I shudder that I may hear the like again. The lady of advanced years could be dead now. Not one but several of the travelling community could be dead or seriously injured. A conviction on all charges must be recorded. It only remains to determine the punishment, which as provided by statute is detention at one of the State's penal institutions.'

The justice peered down at the courtroom and, while renewing with vigour, he appeared overcome or affected by some feeling. His teeth stripped and he smiled in a manner which betrayed inner conflict.

'Were it not for the fact that I doubt the sanity of the accused, Katherine Furlong, I would impose a period of reflection on the perils of propulsory exercise at her age, at the State's hospitality. I give costs against the accused, a fine of ten pounds for the obnoxious weeds and I will apply the probation act in respect of the other charges, provided, Mr Hume, your client consults a qualified and competent psychiatrist within the next seven days.'

Several years prior to this the mother won first prize in a knitting competition. She appeared in the papers as Mrs Kathleen Furlon, Mulgan, County Wicklow. This time she got three full columns, which effectively covered the south-east of Ireland and in addition was featured in what I would call a horror comic printed in Dublin. Her full name, Katherine Aquinas Furlong, widow, farmer, of Mulgannon, Wexford, County Wexford appeared without misprint or misspell. On the same day there appeared a parcel on my breakfast table from Marie Busher. She did not even address me in a courteous manner.

I wish to terminate our relationship at once and I will not attend the Kerlogue beagles on Sunday or anything else at any future date with you because you have made an exhibition of myself and my father in the town. I enclose your Italian record, letter and book on St Augustine and his conversions and I wish to hear no more of the matter or you.

Yours faithfully,
Marie Busher

I thought it was a bit snotty. The only thing that had me worried was the money I had sacrificed on her. I decided that it wasn't me she was after at all but the farm. But be that as it may, I made up my mind never to give impudence to the guards or police in any other country because they are in a very strong position to do you down if they put their minds to it. They are not gentlemen to have as enemies and as the mother pointed out, 'The jury is no place for the fox when the goose is on trial.' The psychiatrist she went to ran her out of the room. He told her that he was nearer fit to be locked up in the asylum himself than she was.

*

I stood in the middle of our yard thinking about the world. There was a wintry gale blowing in from Tuskar. I could see the white foam breaking over Rosslare's banks, and ships scudding in for shelter under the brown cliffs. The wind sent a whip of chaff and short straw to my face. I was thinking about a land I had never seen. It was only fifty miles away as the crow flies yet it was hidden over the horizon – Wales and Britain. I wondered about warm cities and thousands of friendly girls there with huge dance halls and battleships and tanks and planes. I was thinking of going onto a passenger ship like the St David and moving out across Tuskar lighthouse in warmth, in a rich saloon with armchairs and carpets and golden-haired stewardesses in blue uniforms and silk stockings with seams in them and white blouses, moving around asking if there was anything they could do to help and getting into conversation and getting off my mark.

Then there was a voice. A low but distinct voice like a dog's growl, kept at this pitch, no doubt, that the mother wouldn't hear but that I would.

'You're there standing the very same as a monkey trying to get up on a cat. There's ten foot of calf-shit here to be got out and I'm frigged if I'm going to do it on me own. Come on here, God blast you!'

The lean head and shoulders of Moses Flaherty withdrew in from the calf-house window like a scalded snail. I did not like his attitude one bit or suggestions of practices foreign to the Irish way of life. I withdrew indoors. The mother said she was down in herself since the case and that the begrudgers were laughing. I said I had my own troubles and that I could no longer brook Moses Flaherty's vanities.

'The trouble with Mosie Flaherty, Nicholas, is that he doesn't know his place,' the mother said. 'When the working class were hungry they were a hell of a lot better off. There was less impudence out of them. I remember your grandfather in his grand white beard – he'd pass for gentry – standing at the doorway at dinnertime on threshing day, seeing to it that the farmers and their sons went up into the parlour where they belonged for roast beef, and that the farm labourers went where they belonged, down into the kitchen for Rosslare herrings. There was manners on the country in those days. I'm sorry to say they are gone, never to return. Take me down now at once to Nellie MacDonagh in the van, for there's no one better able to take me out of myself. You come along, Nicholas, for you could do with the rest.'

I found the mother more popular in disgrace than when boasting a triumph. Mrs MacDonagh brought us up to the parlour. MacDonagh senior and junior were away and it wasn't long until a full goblet of sherry was in the mother's fist and a glass of lemonade in mine. Nellie MacDonagh held the mother's hand in hers and talked earnestly about 'real tragedies'. While describing disaster, Nellie MacDonagh did not look into my mother's face but all over her clothes and shawl. She kept picking pieces of fluff off them but emphasised points by shaking the mother's clasped hands vigorously inside her own.

'My own born-first cousin, Katie darling, did you hear, dreadful news entirely, declare to God. Here, wasn't she married to a doctor she met at radiography. He made what he liked in Cork city. The children were growing up so he decided to return to Tralee to take up another position. One boy and two girls all brillent, brillent now, Katie. Here, last year didn't the boy, first-class-honours medical student, get in tow with a gambling clique in Cork and stole two hundred pounds out of the Bon Secours hospital and he was destroyed. They don't know where he is. Don't know from Adam where he is this night.'

'You're not in earnest, Nellie MacDonagh,' the mother said.

'He could be in Hong Kong for all they know,' Mrs MacDonagh said. 'The youngest girl, Patricia, was entering the Dominicans. They were mad about her and she was doing speech therapy, a brillent girl. Here now, the letter today, she has gone down with meningitis bad, it would be better if God took her. The second girl is simple of course, and now she's worse.'

'God help the father,' the mother said.

'Drinking like a fish, morning noon and night, and run out of the dispensary,' Mrs MacDonagh said.

'The mother?' the mother asked with profound respect.

'A red, raw, roaring lunatic today in Limerick asylum, Katie Furlong,' said Mrs MacDonagh in proud triumph at her dispatched shock.

The mother took up well after all that and was as gay as a thrush. As she said to me, 'One story is bad until another is told.' She took to going to the pictures and all, stating firmly that we'd all be buried long enough in the bog of Piercestown graveyard. She liked Boris Karloff the best.

8

Rise and Fall

I wasn't going to put any pass on a girl because she had money, no matter how I was provoked by the uncle Dick or the mother. I was surely going to let myself be a bird in a gilded cage. That was all that was on the mother's mind – money and position. If you had money, according to the mother, you could get a woman even if you had a tail, buck teeth and cloven hooves.

'I loved your father, Nicholas,' the mother remarked, 'but he was able to keep me in the manner to which I was accustomed, thanks be to God. If he had not been in a position to do that, and hunger and hardship were my portion, where would love be then?' She smiled bitterly. 'Out the window, hell blast the surer.'

Despite this saturation of delusions about money, the mother succeeded in dooming my ambitions when I had one splendid opportunity. It is about this unfortunate episode that I wish to give an account to the world now. One day, our ailing neighbour Johnny Carty took to the bed. He set the thirty-six acres he owned on conacre. That was a system whereby a person rented the land for eleven months of the year only.

The thirty-six acres were taken by a man described by the mother as the son of 'Knacker Welsh'. The 'Knacker Welsh' the mother referred to had been a strong gentleman of the Barony of Forth, who owned and ran horses at hunts and point-to-point races. His son was none other than George Edward Walshe, a doctor who specialised in heart disease and was so high above the title of doctor that he was properly referred to as Mister Walshe.

Here, however, is the important point. The name spelled 'Walshe' has two pronunciations, both of them correct, but with a difference as subtle as the twitch of a cat's tail. Walshe is pronounced 'Welsh' by riff-raff, corner boys, countrymen and the lower classes. Walshe is pronounced 'Wawlsh' by the gentry, the upper classes, the so-called educated and get-ups.

Specialists have a certain air or grace not enjoyed by the common person. It was the thing to call Mr George E. Walshe 'Mr Wawlsh', a habit the mother picked up without batting an eyelid. She remembered a saying of her grandfather's with regard to footmen: 'Patience must be put on as well as the livery.'

Mr George Edward Walshe contacted Mr Bowe the cattle dealer and engaged him to put into Carty's land forty Aberdeen Angus bullocks. The assignment was duly given to Mr Thomas Boyle, tangler and louser, of whom I have already written a sorry account. In due course there were deposited on Carty's land forty raw cattle, coloured black and bawling with the hunger.

Their demeanour epitomised hazard. It was an emotion swiftly contracted by the mother. In front of our door was a pleasant rectangle of garden, which was tastefully laid out and decorated by Katherine Aquinas Furlong. She regarded this as a more fitting testimonial to the quality of her mind than agricultural production. There were three evergreen trees in it entitled by ribbon *Cyprus Macrocarpa*. There was a selection of ten rose trees, all pruned and trim, with petals of golden, deep red and white hue, as well as a selection in season of daffodil, dahlia, tulip, box plant, lily and the Alpine plant which Mrs MacDonagh brought home to her from Lourdes. There was a tight wire fence separating this artistic enclave from the rest of the field. It was totally adequate to deter our own cattle because the mother struck such terror into their hearts that they shied away from it as if it were a high-voltage wire.

One day the mother looked out the kitchen window. She perceived the open stripped jaws of a straying Walshe bullock vetting the fence into our sweet little meadow. I saw her smiling sadistically at the beast and overheard her address said beast aloud. 'I'd only wish you'd push your head across that ditch until I get the satisfaction of burning you alive.'

A fragrance of delicate blossom stole across Carty's rented land. Every morning in cream jodhpurs with pony jogging came the physician's daughter, Alexandria, to count the bullocks. I opened the gate for her one day and she smiled a brimming smile at me.

'You're a sport, you really are,' she said.

It was a simple sentence. Nevertheless, she said it with such finesse and delicacy that the thought of listening to the horrors slaughtering English filled me with revolt.

The St Martin's Dramatic Society had engaged a great man from the Abbey Theatre in Dublin to conduct a course in elocution. I decided that a cultured tone was a jewel of rare price. I signed on. The elocution lessons provided me with an insight into the horizons of the spoken word. Nevertheless, I considered that I'd heard enough after three lessons to equip myself with the theory for life. We were in our seats in Piercestown Hall when the great man flung open the door and entered, bowing and waving. Prunsheous MacAlla was his name; he was seven feet high, had long hair and wore a sheep fleece around his neck. He addressed us first in Irish, then asked those who understood him to put up their hands. Twelve hands went up out of twenty-one.

'That, ladies and gentlemen,' he said, 'is Lesson Number One. The business of elocution is that one must be clearly understood and heard by all or at least the greatest possible number of one's hearers.'

He grabbed the chalk and inscribed on the board, 'Oh, mother dear, and did you hear the news that's going around?'

'You will appreciate,' he said, 'that there are several different pronunciations of this sentence. For example, upper-class English.'

He wrote again with the chalk and intoned as he wrote, 'Ow, mavva dya, end did you hya va niuuz vats guing wound?'

He continued in west Cork, Dublin and Belfast inter-pretations and then asked us for our own particular version. This evoked much merriment. At my turn, I spoke in plain English that everyone understood – 'Oh, mother dear, and did you hear the news that's going around?'

He considered for a while, then said he didn't think speaking was my *meeteeyay*, paused and guffawed with laughter, slapping his knee. I didn't know what he meant. What care. Everybody concerned with the theatre is half cracked anyhow. I picked up useful tips all the same for future investment.

*

At five o'clock in the bright morning on the very first day of April I was shot to the ceiling of the bedroom with terror. There was an unmerciful shriek from the mother.

'Petrol! Petrol! I'll drench them and burn them alive, the whole God-blasted lot of them.'

I jumped up out of bed, my hair standing on end with the

99

fright. I looked through the window. What I saw was not the panorama of the Irish sea breaking on Rosslare. What I saw was the mild face of a black bullock, from one side of whose jaws protruded the Lourdes Alpine plant, and from the other, a clump of roots and clay, the entire ensemble being shaken vigorously. I opened the door of my room a crack and saw the mother vault down the stairs a-clump-clump-clump-clump, foaming at the mouth, with a horsewhip.

She attacked our meadow and garden single-handed, with shrieks and whip-cracks. It was black with forty close-grazing bullocks. The word got around amongst them that the little woman who was all over the field must have been on a motorbike, for, as one, their tails shot up in stampede formation and off they went, thundering over ditches and hedges, anywhere to get away from the mother and the whip. It took me two days to fence and I had to inform Alexandria that her father's cattle had inadvertently trespassed.

'What a bore, Nicky,' she said. 'Daddy must be told.'

Daddy was told and that very night he drove out in the most gentlemanly fashion and offered ten pounds to the mother in lieu of grass consumed and repairs to fences.

'I am cursed with a rogue beast,' he said.

Mr Wawlshe speaking in English always pronounced the mother's name 'Fairlung'. Not 'Furlon' or 'Furlin' like the uneducated do, or 'Furlong', as pronounced by those of Norman extraction, but 'Fairlung'.

'I am cursed with a rogue, Mrs Fairlung. Could you prescribe a cure? Don't mention that barbarous practice of hanging a car axle out of a beast's neck, dear lady, but is there any other cure? I'm most upset.'

The mother gave her wise, sad smile. 'Oh, indeed, Mr Wawlshe,' she said, 'You've brought the Uncle Tom of Taghmon fame back before me. Yes, there is a cure for roguing and you may keep your ten pounds; what are neighbours for if not to assist one another in peril?'

'That's jolly mature of you I must say, Mrs Fairlung,' remarked Mr Wawlshe.

'The cure for the rogue,' the mother continued with important wisdom, 'is to stitch his two ears together through the lobe, using wax end, and bringing the two ears together on top of his head. Mark my words now, Mr Wawlshe.'

Lo and behold, it was done and it worked. The black rogue bullock had his ears stitched over his head. Without movement, he looked in stupidity at fences the very same as if a magic wand was waved over him. Mr Wawlshe was mad with excitement and he wrote a letter on the experiment to the *Irish Times* and the *Farmer's Journal*. Alexandria asked me to accompany her and her pony, which was entered in the Hickey Perpetual Cup in the Adamstown Show. She came second and when removing the rosette off the bridle she bit her lip and said 'Blawst' three times. It was in that moment of her anguish that I fell in love.

*

It was a mistake to ask the mother. Over to the Wawlshe residence we were both asked for the dinner, although I thought it was very late for that meal. Seven-thirty PM was the time appointed. We usually had our dinner at twelve noon. I spent two days coaching the mother on what to do, what to say and what not to say, for there is nothing more fraught with danger than making a laugh of yourself before the quality. I told the mother that 'I beg your pardon' was more correct than 'Wha'?'

The Wawlshe residence was in the fashionable suburb of Farnogue on the north side of Wexford town, overlooking a pleasant stream. Situated there were the townhouses of the gentry, inasmuch as you can have gentry in a democracy.

We arrived at seven-fifteen and were nearly consumed at the gate by a senile Kerry Blue. Only for where I was I would have issued him with a smart rivet in the bags. The mother looked very well and smelt very well. I saw her put a shot of scent on at the back of her ears. We rang the bell and a servant girl answered the door in a white pinny and cap with lace. Hard on her heels came Alexandria in a cream-coloured thick cloth dress with a belt and buttons, a dark shade of silk stockings and bobbed hair.

She took the mother's coat from her in graceful fashion. She went away with the coat and while she was away we took a quick gander around the hall. In a place of honour, where no one could miss him, was a huge signed photograph of John Edward Redmond, the leader of the Irish Nationalist Party in Westminster at a time when the British had the upper hand here, and dare you say bad was their fashion.

'Ah, will you look at him, God love him,' the mother said with sighed affection. 'Look at him and he up there as proud as a peacock. He died of a broken heart, Nicholas, brought on by the murderers of Ireland.' The mother shook her head.

It was not my place to remind her of the demolition made on the RIC barracks in Murrintown by her brother with a bag of nitrate of soda.

The hall was coated white. A red carpet adorned the floor so thickly that if you fell down you'd smother. The timber of the door, doorcases, hallstand, table and staircase were all a deep and venerable brown and the doorknobs themselves were made of white chaney. On the table was a vase of well-distributed flowers and a big silver gong with a yoke attached, to hit it a belt if the Danes attacked the city.

'The money is falling down off the walls of this house,' the mother declared. 'Where the blasted hell did they get it?' The mother was remembering the time the Wawlshes were not too well acquainted with three meals a day.

'Aw, good day to you, Mrs Fairlung, there you awr now, and how is our young gentleman? My goodness, how chilly it is for May, don't you think so, Mrs Fairlung?'

'It'd skin you, skin you,' said the mother with great intensity. We marched into the presence of Mrs Wawlshe, who was smoking a cigarette through a silver holder. Red lipstick and russet rouge dominated her commendable puss. There was a sideboard packed with silver that would do credit to the shop window of Kerrs the jewellers. This was a big room, and while I remember most of the things in it, especially the old hunting pictures on every wall, I soon had enough action to baffle my memory of such trivialities as furniture.

I regard the use of the French language in restaurants as ignorance. I feel violent on this point. What, therefore, was my reaction when I heard this larded bollocks hurl a French ball across the mother's goalposts and the Christian not settled in her seat?

'*Aperiteefe*, Mrs Fairlung?' His buck-teeth flashed. But the mother was no eejit and hurled a good defensive ball back.

'Why not?' the mother said, not knowing but that it was the *Free Press* she would be handed. What am I talking about? She went from strength to strength and became more chummy and at ease as one sherry after another brought the blush of youth back to her cheeks. She delivered herself to Mrs Wawlshe and Alexandria on a host of topics which varied from the troubles of difficult births, liming land, the Balfour Act and Mr de Valera to the life and times of Pope Pius the Tenth.

'Clear soup you prefer, Mrs Fairlung?' Another ambiguity from Mr Wawlshe which did not deceive the mother, now warmed by her fourth dollop of sherry, which she smartly downed.

'What differ, Mr Wawlshe,' she said.

'There's a marvellous trot for Judy on your fawrm, Mrs Fairlung,' Alexandria remarked.

'Indeed there is, Alexandria,' the mother said, oozing grandeur, 'and I am sick and tired, sick and tired, urging Nicholas Furlong to purchase a gelding to enjoy its advantage.'

After the soup we were given a plateful of fish, and lettuce and sliced eggs in a pink sort of sauce. I thought it was the main feed but we were only getting into our stride. We used the small crooked knives, the same as the Wawlshes. The mother thought the Wawlshes were reverting to their ancestral diets, for she discussed the food value of herrings and that she saw nothing wrong with them. 'Better than a mouthful of snow in the wintertime, Mrs Wawlshe, as the ass said eating the geraniums.'

The next round saw five plates put before us, on whose red-hot surface was deposited a lump of crusty brown steak as big as a turnip with a clump of watercress and two halved tomatoes making a picture as colourful as the Canadian Mounties. A full goblet of red wine was forced upon the mother and everything went on with glee until the heritage of local knowledge and location of birth conspired to throw its acid into the proceedings. The mother had started to brag, using the pontifical plural about our farm and our land steward, Mr Flawrty. A subtlety was launched to put humility on her. Mrs Wawlshe lit a cigarette for herself with her silver flame-thrower. 'Do you keep hunters on your fawrm, Mrs Fairlung?' she asked through a smoke-puff.

The mother smiled affectionately.

'Ah, no, Mrs Wawlshe,' she replied, 'although mind you I often thought of keeping the hounds. But hunters – no, no, I was never a purson myself for the horse or point-to-point racing. Ah no, the dog for me. Give me the greyhound every time. There's one thing about the greyhound. He can't be pulled at the last bend. There's no one riding on his back to do it, you see, and when the trap is up it's nothing else but the red meat on the hare's ribs that occupies his mind, Mrs Wawlshe.'

The mother had driven a sword to the haft in the Wawlshe gizzard. Beads of hot sweat splashed onto my knife. The point-to-point races in Knockhowlin in 1929 were renowned for an event which cost every family in south Wexford serious money. Every family, that is, except the Walshes. Old Knacker Walshe had a grey gelding that could not be passed. He was pulled at the last bend and headed at the post by an ageing cob ranked outside by odds at forty-to-one, the property of a Walshe first cousin. There had been talk of murder.

There descended an abrupt, hostile silence on the room. At last we were all the one. I don't have to tell you any more. I was choking with the pain of the love I had for Alexandria but after that night she wouldn't wipe her boots on me. As a matter of fact she went white with fury every time she saw me in the streets of Wexford town, especially if she was in elevated company.

Of course, she thinks she's the Ascendancy, now that she married a modern veterinary surgeon, the quality in the country today. The Descendancy, if you ask me.

9

UNCLE RICHARD AT DEATH'S DOOR

I went up the hill of Mulgannon with my breath in my fist and broke in on the mother.

'Mother, Uncle Dick has had a heart attack. I heard it only by accident in the Faythe!'

'Is he alive or dead?' the mother asked, turning abruptly up with a frown on her puss.

'He's alive,' I said. 'But there's no hope.'

I didn't know whether I was supposed to have a lump in my throat or be excited, for I found a great attraction in the pageantry which is denied to no man or woman at the assumption of the dignity of corpsehood. In such a demonstration, as next of kin I would play a conspicuous part.

'He was a decent sort of skin at the back of it all,' I said.

The mother placed her right hand up in the air as if forbidding an interruption.

'God send us no greater loss, child,' she said. 'It would be far worse if you were to break a leg.'

A horrible thought tortured the fair garden of her mind. 'Sweet Jesus, I wonder has the crab put pen to paper?' Her doubt spurred an onslaught of panic. 'Get the van at once,' the mother commanded, 'get the van. Down to Poulbrean we'll have to go this very minute, in case the housekeeper wipes your eye.'

She threw every stitch of protective clothing and the old hat she had into a corner. She vanished into the privacy of her own apartments to dress herself in clothes appropriate to the occasion. I went out to see if there was petrol in the van or if it had a flat tyre, for I've noticed that it's at times like this that these trials are sent. When I gave Moses Flaherty, ploughman, the news, he wanted to know if he would go to Piercestown and make a start on the grave. 'You won't have it all your own way either,' Mosie Flaherty said. 'There are great reports about Dick Furlong and a barmaid out in Castlebridge.' I did not pass on his insolence to the mother.

On the way down to Uncle Dick's house, I couldn't help thinking of the fine obituary that could be composed in his favour. He had a very eventful life, and if it was left to me I would draw attention to the many societies – patriotic, cultural and charitable – to which he had made so prolific a contribution.

> Lament him, Learning!
> Science, droop thine head!
> Go! Tell the world around you
> That Richard Furlong is dead.

I would have that for a lead-off. (I got it off a monument to a schoolteacher in the Friary graveyard.)

But to continue my composition.

> The death has taken place at his residence, Poulbrean House, of Mr Richard Furlong. He is survived by his nephew, Mr Nicholas Furlong of Mulgannon, Wexford, and his sister-in-law, Mrs Katherine Furlong, ditto.
>
> He possessed an inexhaustible fund of genial anecdote with which he enriched his hearers.

That sentence is going a bit far. How about this?

> Although not everyone had the good fortune to
> be admitted to the company of his intimate
> friends, those who were, were grappled to his heart
> by hoops of steel. He retained from youth the
> blunt, uncompromising honesty of his Barony of
> Forth stock.

It may occur to some that I have a pongshong for wakes. It is accidental. I merely admit to an obsession for obituaries that dates from the day I was taken by my uncle Dick to see Cavan play Wexford in the All-Ireland football semi-final. That was 1945. I met a boy who was poorly clad and was possessed of an unusual odour. It was in a public house owned by a lady known to the uncle as the Widow Donoghue. This young man was named Mr Ibex and said he was related to a President of Ireland. It was a peculiar name, but then he was in a university for foreigners, namely Trinity College. He introduced me to a guide to writing, entitled *How to Write Obituaries*. It was only two shillings, so I bought it, and it has served me well all my life. While the unlearned have been stuttering to pay tribute to a deceased friend with a boorish, 'Jazes, he was a right man to head the straw rick,' I was always to the fore with a learned remark such as, 'He devoted a long career of unostentatious service to the games and pastimes of the Gael.'

Remarks like this were well received and I became well known for my choice of words on those occasions. My greatest moment arrived at the wake of Nellie MacDonagh's mother, who was eighty-seven and not in her right mind. There was an amount of great mourning and cries, such as is common amongst the Celts. Moses Flaherty remarked while twisting his cap in the wake-room that they were all out of their minds. He was heard to mutter to himself, 'If she was twenty-seven instead of eighty-seven, they'd hang themselves out of ash trees. A mad auld frigger, she should have got the humane killer long ago.'

Before the company had absorbed the significance of these words, I interposed the following in an offhanded manner: 'Nevertheless, she had a veneration for these fountains of classic culture from which she herself had drunk so generously.'

That put manners on the aboriginals.

*

'The smart-arse,' the mother said, brewing vengeance. 'He thought he'd live forever! It's a wonder he didn't cut the briars off the lane before he lost the use of himself.'

We drove past the blackthorns and wild woodbine into the field at the end of which was the long house of the uncle Dick, a good mile from the main road. It suited his own purpose, for he had as much privacy as if he were living in a cocoon. The lights were twinkling in the back windows. There was an air of moment, and sure as hell, when we crossed by the pond we noted that the news had spread. There was one pony and trap, one van like our own and two cars in the yard.

'I declare to God, he's dead,' the mother said. In we walked to the kitchen.

'Ah, here you are at last, his favourite,' said Katie Dempsey, the housekeeper, with tragedy on her face. She consulted the mother's eyes. 'I thought you'd be here hours ago,' Miss Dempsey continued in defensive attack, 'but I wasn't going to send you word until there was a change.'

The mother threw her eyes around the kitchen. There were cousins there from the four branches surviving – the Codds of the Moor, the Doyles of Lambstown, the Donoghues of the Old Pound and the Whittys of Waterford. The sight of the last-named nearly stopped the mother's heart, for they had travelled fifty miles and we were only four miles away. Worse was registered against the mother's eyes. Underneath the Sacred Heart lamp, the mother identified the brazen presence of the barmaid from Dillon's of Castlebridge. The mother controlled herself by holding Miss Dempsey the housekeeper by the hand and asking, 'Are we to be prepared for the worst?'

'Come on,' the housekeeper said, nodding to the bedroom. 'He's had the priest. He's been anointed.'

The mother made no enquiry as to legal arrangements. She nodded in sorrow to the other relations who had arrived before her and who looked as full as eggs.

'We'd a puncture on the way,' she whispered.

The two of us crept in. He was there with his eyes wide open, on the pure white-laced pillow, staring at the ceiling in boredom. I considered the great body weighed down by a lifetime of service to his fellow countrymen, the great mind, ever unselfish to the point of foolishness in the dissemination of ideas, both now slipping into the vortex, and from this vortex, unlike the others in his life, there would be no return.

I briefly considered his many contributions to learning, the arts and science, which have since borne fruit. Was he not the first man to suggest a Wexford Festival, only to become the butt of loafers' remarks? Was he not the man who advised Brother Holland, who was teaching in Enniscorthy, that it was time someone constructed a submarine boat? Was it not he who stated that the New Ross, Edermine and Wexford bridges comprised white elephants? The answer to all of these questions is, 'He was.'

The mother turned to the housekeeper.

'Have you got the habit?'

The housekeeper, Katie Dempsey, gazed at her as if she'd got a belt of a wet mackerel. She said nothing. The mother dispersed her ignorance with contempt.

'If the habit is placed over the feet of the dying person at the time of approaching death, he receives a special indulgence,' she said and approached the catafalque.

It was not a cheerful sight. The great girth of Richard Furlong covered in its entirety the simple bed. The sixty-five per cent wax candles flickered against the wall. The low murmur of his cousins saying the rosary was broken by the occasional wild sob of Dillon's barmaid, a feature of the approaching end of all great Celtic chieftains. A plain white sheet covered his frame. There was a slight commotion as the rest of the family, satisfied that every stick in the house had been noted, gathered up to the bedroom.

Richard Furlong was restored momentarily to clarity.

'Bring them all in, Katie Dempsey,' he said. 'And treat them decent, as befits the house of Furlong.'

The mother moved up to the head of the bed and put her hand on his. 'Oh, Uncle Richard,' said she. 'You look far, far better. I think there's an improvement. Isn't there something about the face and eyes now, Katie, don't you think? Yes, there's definitely a change.'

The change the mother wished for was a whitening of eye and a stopping of breath, for it was held that he had the weight of himself in gold and hadn't spent a rash shilling for thirty years – all provided, of course, that I, the next-of-blood-kin, was the written, signed and certified beneficiary.

'No, no,' said the uncle. 'It is the end. I only wish it could be for Ireland.'

Nellie Codd of the Moor put in her spoke where it wasn't asked or called for.

'Richard,' said she, instead of trying to keep his heart up, 'Richard, have you any last message for us all on your dying bed?' Her voice quavered with remorse, for she had smashed a full whiskey bottle over his head after the Civil War. The mother said afterwards that it was a wonder she didn't vomit over the sick man when she heard her.

'Yes, I have a message,' he said quietly. 'I have a message for the world. Mark it well.'

He summoned every vestige of his ebbing strength, raised himself up on his elbows and rose his voice to an apoplectic bellow of rage.

'Beware of the begrudger!'

The windows rattled, the candle flame flapped wildly and the sheepdog ran howling across the fields like a shot fox.

He fell back on the pillow with a slump, exhausted.

The dark warning and the manner of its delivery had a great impact on his nearest and dearest.

The mother with deliberate intent issued the following. 'How, Richard Furlong, are we to know the begrudger?'

The uncle came to and fixed clear eyes on the mother. In normal tones he said, 'I'm very glad you asked me that question, for I've yet some more to add.'

A dark expression flooded every crevice of his face.

'First of all, I will tell you what the begrudger is not. He or she is not the one flushed with hate and venom who wouldn't bid you the time of day. The begrudger is not the one who goes out of his or her way to thwart you in your objectives in life. Here is not the begrudger. Here is manifested – and since observed is harmless – a commodity known as the bester.'

The uncle here indicated by signs that he was parched. A full tumbler of a white, smoky liquid was presented to him, which he gurgled back unaided. An expression of introspection indicated by a narrowing of the eyelids claimed the great man. His voice lowered. 'The begrudger is the one who falls over you with good cheer and hospitality, will even persuade you of exceptional qualities you haven't got . . . ' Again he rose up on his elbow, again he roared, in full cannon blast, ' . . . in order to speed you on to your own destruction!'

He became subdued as the memory of a great wrong receded. Low-voiced, he continued, 'The begrudger is a bosom friend, who in Council stands by you. Whether that council is County Wexford's, the Knights of Columbanus, party branch, the Vincent de Paul, unemployment exchange, dispensary, board of directors, bar or crossroads, is immaterial. When your name comes forward for consideration, he will say with a friendly smile, "There's no one I'd sooner have at my side, himself and myself are inseparable – even though there might be a bit of history there."'

At this stage the uncle Dick's face could clearly be seen, against the starched white pillow, to turn a shade of purple. Froth bubbled at the corner of his mouth. 'This means,' said he, in a voice trembling with passion, 'that *you are insane*, and that, when the steam is turned on, you will stampede to an attic over the Slaney to cut paper dollies out of news-papers.'

He shut his eyes and the mourners took advantage to gaze at one another, as a microbe of familial insecurity set in.

'But even he is not the most dangerous begrudger,' continued the uncle Dick. 'Do you realise that destruction may be wreaked upon your ambition, without one word being spoken?'

'How could that be, Richard Furlong, now?' Nellie Codd asked, right interested.

'I can recall an occasion when a certain person sent his name forward for responsible employment.'

Here the uncle choked, but resumed with clearly worded severity after a further libation. 'As soon as the name came up, the applicant's best friend, companion and sponger simply nodded his head, smiled knowingly and started to drum his fingers on the table.'

The uncle smiled and drummed his fingers loudly upon his own bed table. He roared, 'This meant that the party mentioned had fingers trained to empty the till!'

He became delirious. In a low babble, almost as if chanting a litany, he drummed on. 'Begrudgers everywhere. Begrudgers upstairs, downstairs, to the right and to the left, in the church and in the ballroom. I'm surrounded by begrudgers to the last. *Begrudgers!'*

I got the bottle of spirits and forced it between his teeth, gripping him by the nostrils like a bullock. I gave him a good drench of it and brought a blush back to his cheeks.

'The devil a much is wrong with Dick Furlong,' the mother said. 'I'm ten times worse myself.'

The uncle gave in to a pleasant slumber and snored in a normal healthy fashion.

Frank Whitty, who had travelled from Waterford to assist at the last respects, was over six feet tall and a very agreeable sort who made a fortune out of selling motorbikes to cattle jobbers and the sons of gentlemen. He was able to get off his mark with any girl he liked and often told me about them.

'All you want,' he told me, 'is the technique. Women are the very same in the middle of the night if they had a bag over their heads.'

I thought that this was a sweeping generalisation but I

was conscious of a glimmer of truth in it.

We moved out of the bedroom. Frank Whitty turned to Katie Dempsey and passed a civil remark to the effect that there were a lot of rushes in the place.

'Two acres of rushes out of a hundred is not to be despised, Mr Whitty,' said Katie.

'One hundred acres! Mother of God, my mother told me that there was an acre here for every day of the year. Three hundred and sixty-five, no less. What did you do with them?' Frank asked in alarm.

'We didn't bury them in the quarry hole, Mr Whitty,' said Katie in defiance and not another word did she add to that.

The mother gave me a puck in the ribs. She nodded her head to indicate flight and, without a civil word to a living Christian but a death wish on Dillon's barmaid, she withdrew from the house.

'Richard Furlong will live to be ninety, Nicholas, and he'll thwart you yet,' the mother said on the way back. 'He can't be trusted.'

The purist will now say that this chapter has no place in an account of the snares lurking in pursuit of a suitable match. This attitude shows feeble powers of perception. With the wind of the uncle Dick in my back, position, credit and prestige would advance me far towards an acceptable matrimonial alliance. No woman in her right mind would cross the threshold to share life with me and the mother. The position was, without the Poulbrean estate I was as inviting as a cat with the scurvy.

The uncle recovered to win a step-dance competition six weeks later in Butlers of Lady's Island. The developments injected in Moses Flaherty the instinct for further agitation. The mother was the audience he wanted.

'Do you think Dick Furlong of Poulbrean is right in the head, ma'am?' he asked, while busy but not facing her.

'What's he at now?' the mother asked, and she all stiffened up.

'Well, you'd hear an odd thing here and there. Do you know that he hires Taxi Brien to take himself and the barmaid in Dillon's of Castlebridge down to Rosslare Strand every Thursday, the half day? There could be a settlement there yet and a houseful of children. That one is only thirty. You could hardly blame the Christian. A single man in a big house and a big farm. He must be going queer with the lonesomeness.'

A spectre intruded upon the mother's mind. The abuse of her mental arrangements resembled the meshing of steel gear cogs. The engine of her brain stopped. She turned and retired in silence to the kitchen. Mosie Flaherty was not content unless he added to the same intelligence for my benefit.

'I'm telling you, my boy, when Dick Furlong lays his big cold hand on that one's belly in the middle of the night, be hell she'll leap up in the air as high as the ceiling.' He carried on then with another sort of tune to play.

'You'd better go down and see that raving stallion more often instead of standing up here scratching your bags. Make up to him. Bring him down a naggin of whiskey. Then, as soon as he makes the place over to you, you could get a friendly nurse or a doctor to give him a shot of the needle, and fare you well Dick Furlong.'

I did not like one bit being taken to be an entire loon by the likes of Moses Flaherty.

10

THE FOREIGN GAME

Mulcahy was saturated in his violence. The gentlemanly behaviour for which he and his family were famed was scattered like chip bags at a greyhound track. It was all very fine to be put off the pitch by the referee in the heat of the struggle. At least it carried with it the esteem and sympathy of the club. It was quite another matter when the referee's report on the game was read to the district committee and published in full in the *Wexford Free Press*. It appeared on the opposite page to that which carried the subscriptions to the annual collection of the St Vincent de Paul Society, upon which Joseph G. Mulcahy senior, Mulgannon House, was featured leading the poll with twenty golden guineas. The reporter was the know-all Gilroy.

HOOLIGANISM WILL BE STAMPED OUT
REFEREE'S REPORT ADOPTED

'There is no place in our national games for the violence we have seen in recent months, and, while I am chairman, I will see to it that hooliganism will be stamped out.'

So stated Mr Aodh Latimore, chairman of the Wexford District Board of the GAA at its meeting last Monday night when the referee's report on the junior hurling championship game between the St Fintan's and the Erin Hopes was adopted by sixteen votes to two.

The referee, Mr James Kelly, stated in his report that the game was conducted in a sporting manner until five minutes before half-time, when the St Fintan's goalie was injured following an invasion of the goalmouth. The goalie had to be replaced in the second half. It was impossible for him (Mr Kelly) to see which player had caused the injury to the goalie.

On the resumption of play the game was carried on in a sporting manner, but in the sixteenth minute the St Fintan's centre-back, E. Grace, assaulted the Erin Hopes' right corner-forward, N. Furlong. The injury to the Erin Hopes corner-forward necessitated his removal from the field. He was replaced by S. Cogley. Following the above-mentioned assault, the Erin Hopes full-back, Mulcahy, ran the full length of the field and assaulted the St Fintan's centre-back, E. Grace. The referee dismissed both players from the field. During the remainder of the game he was subjected to unwarranted barracking by supporters of both sides, and at the end of the game he was approached by a playing official of the St Fintan's club and called 'a blind —.' Had the St Fintan's official and supporters not been restrained, an ugly situation would have developed, he stated.

The players sent off were Joseph Mulcahy (Erin Hopes) and Edmond Grace (St Fintan's). The offending official was named as Mr John Lambert (St Fintan's).

Mr John Lambert (St Fintan's) responded. 'On a point of order, Mr Chairman, I did not refer to Mr Kelly as 'a blind —.' It was after the match anyhow. I wanted to say to him that if he was up with the play he could have done justice in the first half if he wasn't blind. I did not use the language the referee mentioned in his report. All I have to say is that if the match he's talking about is the way hurling is going to go, then God help Wexford. Neither me nor Mr Rowe will vote on accepting that report, which is a negation of democracy.'

Mr Charles Fitzgerald (Erin Hopes): 'The referee did a good job of refereeing and the one time the thing boiled up he quickly brought the thing to its senses by sending a player off from both sides. It was a good sporting game and we would like to compliment the referee and officials. The St Fintan's have a good team and if they train they will go far next year. The Erin Hopes look forward to meeting them again.'

The referee's report was adopted on the proposition of Anthony Saunders (St John's Volunteers), seconded by Brendan Corcoran (Castlebridge), by sixteen votes to two. Having made the remarks quoted at the outset, the chairman ruled that the two players, Joseph Mulcahy junior and Edmond Grace, be suspended for two calendar months. A similar period of suspension was imposed on the St Fintan's official, John Lambert.

'The old man is fit to be tied,' said Mulcahy, with neurosis tearing his guts.

I did my best to patch him up. I laughed at his father and his scandalised rugby brothers with their notions of good manners. His sister and mother were delighted that he was able to stand up for himself.

'His was a brave deed,' said Mrs Mulcahy.

'Thermopylae again,' the sister said.

'You mean Pearl Harbour,' said Mr Mulcahy senior. 'Let him take up a sport where the game's the thing and not fisticuffs.'

Mulcahy's heart and independence were sucked out of him. I wouldn't mind, but he was big enough to ravish the whole parish. But the distaste in which his dismissal from the field, plus its publicity, was held by his family seeped into Mulcahy like a fog.

'Shag the GAA. I'll give hockey a try.' Mulcahy made the decision. It was a decision as gulf-forming as emigration, for between the Gaelic Athletic Association and the rugby, cricket, soccer and hockey codes there was an antipathy of racist proportions. The others were predominantly British garrison sports when this country was under the White Raj.

In south Wexford, the Greenfield club was comprised in the main of farmers' sons and their sisters with Norman names and notions. The Wexford club was comprised of urban players of all races and creeds leavened with a sprinkling of loud, vociferous ex-officer and landed-gentry types.

I happened to mention to the mother that Mulcahy was thinking of going over to hockey. She smiled wisely. 'Ah, yes, Nicholas, I was waiting for that. I knew in my heart of hearts that something better than association with the commonality would be arranged for Master Mulcahy. Mrs Mulcahy is the full of herself.'

'Well, smart and all as you are, you're wrong. It was old Joe Mulcahy that won't let him play GAA any more,' I said with vexation.

'Mr Mulcahy would sound better in your mouth, Nicholas,' the mother said, 'and he is no bite-the-wall either; as God made them, he matched them. It would be no harm if you joined him. I notice that in this part of the country, the quality, or if you prefer, those who have the security of land or cash or both at their backs, are to be found playing hockey. Contradict me, Nicholas, if I'm telling a lie.'

'You surely don't want me to trot out with that dolt Westroppe for the foreign game,' I said, 'the game that was played when patriots were marched up the gallows.'

'Over the last six hundred years,' the mother said, 'seventeen Furlongs marched up the thirteen steps and none of them came down on their own feet. I don't recall,' she went on, 'the clink of coin into our cash box from a grateful country in token of their sacrifice. I'm sick and tired of telling you to watch your company and to mix around with respectable boys and girls. The Eiryann Hopes,' the mother sing-songed contemptuously. 'The Eiryann Hopes! The Eiryann Despairs would be better. Scruff, the whole lot of them.'

I was getting a bit sick now of learning about the Furlongs who were hanged and the Furlongs who were shot at the siege of Ross. I didn't want to remind her of the six who were hanged because they hung lanterns around cows' necks and drove them down the strand of Kilmore until a four-master was wrecked.

I said I'd go. I said it to myself because I didn't want to discuss my business with the mother. I resolved to go with Mulcahy when I reflected on the way I was dropped from the Erin Hopes after I had offered my life while in my sins.

But there was a decision to be reached. On which team was it the best on all counts to play hockey?

I could see the hand of fate interfering once more. I was in love. Deeply, heart-wrenchingly in love. The first time I had seen her was when I was minding cattle at the fair of Wexford, at the bottom of Hill Street. She was going to school in the Loreto Convent. She was clad on that warm day in her school uniform, a dark-brown gym frock, white blouse, red sash around the waist and a Legion of Mary medal on a blue ribbon. She had light-brown silk stockings and flat brown shoes. She had blonde hair. The soft waves fell over her right eye and she occasionally brushed them back with her hand. She was not just pretty. She was beautiful. She had a beauty of self-assurance and kindness and feminine knowledge and distinct character. She was tall and her skin was fair. I thought of angry sermons on immodest dress and modern fashions. Yet here was a girl in total modesty and I would have willingly thrown myself off the spire of Bride Street to please her.

The fair vanished, the cattle, the curses, God-blasts and shouts of the dealing men. I saw her only as a kind sun spotlighted her. She must come by me. She must have felt me. As she came close she looked at me and I could not switch my eyes off. We both looked and she blushed to her blonde hair. Then she was gone. I found out with feverish haste through Mulcahy who she was. She lived in Rowe Street with her daddy, who was medical officer of health with the county council. I went to thorough pains to find out where she went, what she was interested in, what Mass she went to. I tossed myself deliberately but discreetly in her way. Since she was a woman she must have known that I loved her, for shortly after she began to turn a shy smile to me. This was always preceded by a frown, but on recognition her face opened and a sunburst of happiness engulfed it.

She played hockey with the Wexford town club. Simple problem for the gallant lover? Not at all. I knew I wasn't good enough for her, but why dwell on that unhappy gulf. If I joined the Wexford town hockey club it would have been clear that I was flinging myself at her and therefore a sticking-plaster nuisance. If, on the other hand, I joined Greenfield, I would be among kindred Barony-of-Forth farmers, poor but proud, and I would be visiting and playing Wexford at their Rosemount grounds at least four times every year. Since men's teams and girls' teams always made up the double fixture, I could engage without inappropriate suspicion in proximity to my only love, Celia Brennock. But Greenfield was eight miles away from Mulgannon, and Wexford's Rosemount grounds were only three. The situation was fraught with delicacy.

I went down to Mulcahy, taking pains to avoid Mr Mulcahy senior, whom I feared and whom I suspected regarded me as an idler. I addressed Mulcahy, who was involved in washing the family car.

'I think I'll play hockey.'

Mulcahy cheered up and worked himself up to a beam.

'Yeah?' he said.

'I have given long and serious thought to the matter. I'm afraid we may not be together.'

'Why not?' asked Mulcahy.

'Well, to tell you the truth, I'm worried about the Wexford club. I've been secretly told that the players are not of our race. I'm all for friendly relations, but if you got involved maybe it's lose the religion we have already. I knew a girl some time ago in Enniscorthy . . . '

'Who the hell said I was going to join Wexford?' barked Mulcahy.

'I thought . . . '

Mulcahy swallowed a stream of vulgarities, flung a bucket of water at the car and swore he wouldn't be caught dead in the Wexford hockey club.

'Thank God for that anyhow,' I remarked and withdrew to think.

I was not immediately picked to play for the Greenfield club. The captain, Dan Browne, told me that I'd be brought to a few games and that I was to keep my eyes open until I got the hang of it. That very week, thanks be to the Mother of sweet God, we were playing Wexford at Rosemount in the south-east league. Over to those semi-heretical environs I went with joy stifled in my mouth. Mulcahy of course had no difficulty in getting a place in the back division. We drove in through the gates of Rosemount. Foreign cries such as 'Sticks, sticks!' smote my ear. The refined expression floated across the field like a ballet frock. Old Major Westroppe, a busy little man with a moustache and khaki army coat, was marching up and down with an important slip of paper, summoning a scatter of hockey players together.

There were irreverent criticisms voiced by members of the Greenfield club suggesting immoral practices by members of the Wexford club. I challenged one remark and was informed by one John Joe Howlin that the auld frigger in the uniform was in jail in Africa for ten years on a charge of unnatural bestiality. I became very nervous but I ignored the trend of the conversation. I had spotted Celia.

I crossed to where she was playing, just to watch her. On the way I passed maidens of all shapes and dispositions displaying their persons on the warm grass with pleasing frivolity. I asked myself if I was out of my mind to be in the Gaelic Athletic Association. Then I caught Celia's eye in a while and she smiled a greeting very shyly.

After her girls' match was over there was a bit of a practice and I was given a hockey stick by old Major Westroppe himself. I informed him I was new. He pranced around in a tweed hat with the rim down around his ears.

'Couldn't start younger. Out with you. Run like a hare and position yourself for a pawce.'

The ball came across to me and I swung onto it at once with a whop. It was like a mug of concrete and it whizzed by the goal like a rocket, bringing a big girl's specs with it and almost parting Celia's hair. I was petrified. Cries such as 'Stupid awss' and 'Demn sevege' were proclaimed. These were hard words for me to bear. Apart from Celia being nearby to hear them, I was the descendant of a line of landed gentry in possession, as Senator Kathleen Browne wrote in her famous history, of noble blood.

I had a bar of chocolate in my pocket and a bag of jellies. I gave the unopened bag of jellies to Celia very shyly. I told her to please take it because I was sorry I had frightened her. She looked at me for a long time while nursing the bag. Then I experienced an exchange of feelings, but she and I were constrained by a shyness that reduced words to drivel. She just said that I was very thoughtful. Then I had to tear my eyes and presence away.

The men's match was a violent affair, as bad if not worse than the Erin Hopes–St Fintan's confrontation. There was much recourse to the Holy Name amid elemental Celtic and West British contumelies. This was particularly noticeable at the time of lost chances. Eventually at close of play the score was Wexford 2, Greenfield 2; a draw.

That night I waited for a party in the clubhouse for the visiting team, to wit, ourselves, Greenfield. There was tea and ham sandwiches and all sorts of scones and cake and a ten-gallon milk-churn full of draught Guinness for those who needed the alcoholic stimulant. Despite much bawdy laughter and intermingling of the races where drinking to excess reduced all barriers, there was a refined atmosphere among those who did not sully their lips with the Bacchanalian drop.

Mulcahy was in his element and gave full expression to his delightful manners, which endeared him to opponents of both sexes. Not a crumb crossed his lips until he was satisfied that firstly, every lady had her share, and secondly, every non-drinking gentleman had his share, seated. Beaming, he remarked on the refinement of the gathering – so different from others in which he had mixed. There were frequent enquiries about his parents' health and about his brother's achievement in his finals. Mulcahy behaved with a grace in this atmosphere which made me contemplate with pleasurable anticipation his reaction to the occasion when one of the gentry would sweep the kneecap off him with a belt of a hockey stick.

I worked myself around with craft to Celia's side of the room, where, amid a suggestion of perfume, she was filling cups of tea. She gave me a cup and sat beside me. She said she knew I was a farmer. She was doing a project for the nuns in her school on agriculture and was fascinated.

It is extraordinary how the harsh life is smothered in the mystique of soil science, fresh air, blossoms in May and the involvement in the life process. She was intensely impressed and we went on to discuss religion and politics and systems of government and women's points of view, a subject on which I was well equipped to hold forth.

She had but one dread and that was drink. There was no problem here since I was a total abstainer but she regarded anyone who drank with a disgust and a venom which I thought was alarming in one who possessed so angelic a persona.

There was at this juncture a hullabaloo raised. Men with pint-smears on their lips and sparkling eyes called for concert items. I redeemed my little lapse on the field of play by rendering the 'Charge of the Light Brigade' with actions. I was the recipient of hearty congratulations from many well-wishers, not the least of whom was Major Westroppe, who had taken a shine to me. He gave me a copy of a poem named 'Gunga Din' with a request that I learn that off too. Although he wasn't an African himself, he had been in the Royal Uganda Rifles for twenty-five years.

Celia and I began to be thrown in one another's way. There was a monster hockey tournament for beginners arranged in Dublin. It was decided to send a mixed team of junior players from Wexford and Greenfield, to play a similiar combination from Grangegorman Hospital. Celia was picked and old Westroppe shouted, 'Try Furlong. Young chap. Trier all the way.' I was on.

A fortnight later we set out for the grounds belonging to Grangegorman Hospital in Dublin. Mulcahy brought his daddy's car, a thing he never got to transport the Erin Hopes. He also collected Celia and I engineered it so that she was in the front seat between Mulcahy and me. I was stomach-puffed in love and I played with her on the way up. The back seat was occupied by Danny Browne, who was travelling as a mentor, John Joe Howlin and a fine agricultural girl from Greenfield.

The fact that I was engaged in conversation of uplifting level with Celia didn't suit them. Master Mulcahy suggested, 'Nicholas should be formulating plans to deceive the opposing team,' accompanied by a condescending smile. I resolved that in a moment of confusion on the field of play, if Mulcahy were involved, I would hit him a root in the bum and run like stink before he saw who did it.

The Glen of the Downs was reserved by the unlettered for an onslaught on propriety. Howlin and Browne had slaughtered several gins and pints in Ashford. They coughed loudly as we went through the Glen. Mulcahy opened his mouth and uttered an unscholarly 'Wha'?'

Howlin said, 'Mr Browne and I would like an occasion to answer a call of nature.'

The lack of delicacy in which Celia was drenched affected me in unbidden blushes. Browne kept insisting that I was in need of joining them. In order to spare Celia vulgar expressions, I joined them in the laurel trees. John Joe Howlin put forward advice on how I might fulfil my affection. I did not like his attitude, nor did I need or invite his advice. He said he only offered it because he was often on the same tack himself. Tack is a word common in rural areas. It has no association of a noble or pure nature unless one is referring to manoeuvres at sea.

We drove on. Danny Browne in the back seat commenced to give advice. He informed us that the Grangegorman players were all mental and that the club was got together so that the members could work off their insanity. This intelligence was challenged by myself, Mulcahy and Celia.

'All right,' said John Joe Howlin, 'don't believe Browne, but wait till you see the bugger marking Furlong.'

'What's wrong with him?' I asked.

'Nothing's wrong with him,' replied Howlin, 'except that he wears rings in his two nostrils,' and so saying folded his arms and slapped back in his seat as if he had announced the outbreak of war.

'The curse of hell on the lie,' added Danny Browne.

Sure enough, when we arrived on the pitch, what did I see but a thin Irishman with grey hair, about five feet ten in height, and dangling out of his nose were two plain but wide and shiny gold rings.

'I told you, didn't I?' said Howlin. 'They're all insane, every single one of them.'

I resolved to watch myself first and Celia second, so that serious injury or molestation of any kind would not be our portion. Old Westroppe came bounding out of a rusty vehicle that looked far worse than our own van at home. It did not have a humiliating effect on him, however.

'Aw! There you are, Furlong, lively and well! Did you bring Gunga Din?'

'I think, sir,' I said civilly, 'there are enough Gunga Dins up here.'

He thought this remark entertaining. Roared like a buffalo and shouted, 'Bless my soul! Chap's right!'

The Grangegorman Hospital mixed juniors came out onto the field in red shirts. They looked normal. Too normal. If they had looked a bit queer, I wouldn't have minded half as much. Sure enough, there was your man with the noserings looking calm, chatting politely about the weather and picking up a fallen hockey stick belonging to a maiden and handing it to her. I did not feel fright, but a feeling stole over me of being in a world where something queer might be expected at any minute.

Old Westroppe came over before I went out on the field. He said I looked washy. 'The drive, no doubt. Drink this.' I drank a deep draught from a silver flask he carried around his back. It had a strong, sweet peppermint flavour and was so hot that it took the linings off my throat. 'Good for the wind,' he said. I trotted off, a new man after the major's beverage. Celia had engaged in chat with a tall fellow who looked to have nothing but marble north of his Adam's apple. It was an old friend, she told me, who was a fruit company executive.

There were three things I didn't latch on to about hockey. One is that you can't bury the goalie in the back of the net. The second thing is that you can't run into the forward scoring area before the ball arrives. Thirdly, there are two referees, one for each side of the pitch. This last arrangement was my undoing because I resolved to do an Erin Hopes on the danger to Celia. I resolved to sicken with a belt the banana man who was put out to mark my intended.

The only unnerving thing about the match was the man with the noserings who was marking me. He passed many observations on the weather, thus testifying to his healthy mind. I calmed down. Then, occasionally, the sun made his noserings glitter. I became winded trying to play him, outwit him and at the same time keep a respectable distance. I was never under such fatigue before and, as I waited to recover after one bright dispatch of play near the sideline, out rushed old Westroppe, flushed and wildly exhorting the players. He whipped the flask from his shoulder.

'Head up, Furlong, down the bloody hatch, the lot!' I drank about a gallon of it and, when I straightened up, sparks and black dots cascaded over my eyeballs. I felt a furnace in my stomach which flooded every vein right down to my toes. And then my main chance appeared. There was a forward attack. I saw Celia move forward to score while the banana man who was marking her rushed back to defend on the goal line.

I took off. The referee was nowhere in sight and I tore into the main adversary with butt of stick, knees and all. The whole issue, including three backs, a spectator, Celia, myself, the female goalie and the ball, ended up in the back of the net. In the process I received a savage blow on the bridge of the nose.

The spectator disentangled himself, put a whistle into his mouth and blew ten riot blasts with unbridled fury pumping through his veins. 'Saw nothing like it since Singapore,' he blurted.

Major Westroppe did a dance of joy.

'That's the spirit, Furlong! All the way back! Nil desperandum!'

But I was disgraced once more. The spectator was really referee number two.

I didn't think it was right for Celia to say I was drunk. I was only trying to save her life and it was no fault of mine that my Confirmation pledge had been outwitted. My nose was broken but it would be company for my heart. That night at the reception, Celia succeeded in turning my stomach. She didn't just ignore me. She accepted entertainment in the banana man's lap. She danced with him, looking into his eyes as if he were the Dalai Lama. On his club jacket there shone a pioneer badge.

I thought I might as well be hanged for a sheep as a lamb. I joined Major Westroppe, who prescribed gin for my stomach and the pain, with strong doses of black stout to wash it down.

I spent time discussing racial prejudice with Major Westroppe. He honoured me with certain confidences. He informed me that the women of central Africa, especially in the French colonies, were intellectually superior to any white woman. He also informed me that the longer one was in Africa, the whiter the women became.

That night I was delivered home to Mulgannon in a state of ossification. I was brought only as far as the bend of the road. Mulcahy, who did not speak to me on the return journey, said that he would not face Mrs Furlong at the moment of my disgrace.

'That,' I replied, 'is your business and your privilege. As for myself, I wish to thank you for the favour of your company and that of the entire car. Here's to a better day. I now follow the path trodden by every generation of my family. I will walk with head erect into my own house at a time of my own choosing and no matter how much more it will be, it will certainly never be no less.'

I went in the front door on my hands and knees. I remember but dimly my reception. I remember being described as a blasted full-bellied ruffian and Antichrist. My last recollection is that of my person kneeling down on the kitchen floor with my two arms outstretched before the Sacred Heart picture, repeating after the mother the words of the pledge to give up drink for life in honour of the Thirst and Passion.

The next morning I left without breakfast to weed beet in the big Carraigun field. I fell down in the drills and vomited my whole body up. I recited in all sincerity the following prayer: 'O Almighty God, I have not troubled You with my demands in this life. I'm entitled to some favour. Take me home to Yourself this day. Amen.'

11

DESTROYED FOR LIFE

My nose was broken. There was a dull pain all over my face. If I closed one eye I could see the grotesque bulge of the nose as it was pushed over to the left side of my face. The mother was very upset and said I was destroyed for life. Between crying and abuse, I didn't know what to make of her.

'Go down,' she said, 'to Dr Devereux. He's the only doctor in town for a cur like you. Jesus, Mary and Joseph, amn't I rightly hoaxed up?'

I went down and joined the patients in Dr Devereux's waiting room at Magdalen House. It was a very interesting waiting room, packed with magazines and guns and swords. There was a huge bookcase with glass windows. It contained all sorts of exciting books on history and everything under the sun. I was surely three hours there when I was called in. I was very much afraid, because this man had only two moods, very good and very bad. He was seated behind a big desk, a low-sized man with a thick wad of greying black hair brushed back. He had thick, bushy eyebrows which peered down over his ashen face. He chewed a large pipe with vigour while slowly shuffling medical cards.

'What's wrong with you?' he asked, without looking at me.

'I've a broken nose, doctor,' I said.

His eyebrows dived into a clinch and his wide eyes searched my face.

'How the hell do you know you've a broken nose?'

I was very put aback by this question. I volunteered that I'd never heard of anyone having a sprained nose.

He removed the pipe from his mouth. 'It is not unknown for an impudent pup to have a sprained arse,' he said. 'Who are you, anyhow?'

I gave him my name and my address.

'Is your mother the one who lives in the last house up that road?'

'Yes, doctor,' I said, brightening up in view of the fact that the mother impressed him with her personality. 'Do you know the mother?'

'I do,' he said. 'She owes me money. Come over here until I see that nose.'

I went forward with truculence. He looked at it and I noticed the unusual smell of the tobacco he smoked. He placed his finger on my nose. The pressure was not great but he touched a nerve, for a red coal of pain shafted through my head. I emitted a roar in proportion to the pain.

'*Aaawwwwwwyow!*'

'You goddamn son of a bitch,' he startled back, 'you'd think I was after shoving a knife in you to the melt. It's broken.'

He kept studying it.

'That is most interesting,' he said. 'Most interesting.'

I made so bold as to enquire what was most interesting.

'It is exactly the injury, in exactly the spot that I inflicted upon two of the Worcestershire Regiment who thought that they had me. If the nose is struck in an upward trajectory, it can result in death.'

My eyes opened wide. He noted the interest, tapped the ash out of his pipe and proceeded to fill it again out of a light-coloured purse. 'Of course,' he said, 'they had no respect unless you were every damn bit as good to kill as they were. I sent a few of them to the happy hunting ground. I had to bury two of them in Hutchisons' land in Coolballow and I noticed that the grass grew there afterwards just the same.' He gave a curious throat-chuckle, then he peered at me.

'What about the men with noses you broke, doctor?' I asked, with great admiration for the many blows for freedom which had been struck by the one man.

'That was in Cleariestown. I was holed up there with Fintan Howlin of Duncannon. We were on the run and our ammunition was running out. Fintan had a Thompson gun and I had a Mauser and a parabellum.'

I must have looked at him in ignorance.

'Here to hell, I'll show you.' He opened up a big case and took out a heavy revolver with a long barrel. He looked at it fondly. 'As good as a rifle,' he said. 'Never let me down. That's a parabellum.'

'You were in Cleariestown,' I said.

'Out in Scallans' house,' he said. 'We stopped only the one night. But some bastard must have tipped off the barracks in Wexford because at daybreak there was a roar of engines and two Crossley tenders came into the yard. I didn't wait for them to settle their feet on the ground. I raked the place with bullets and Fintan did the same from another window. We bagged ten men and the rest got down behind the haggard wall to say their prayers. We exchanged rapid fire until there were only three of them left and our ammunition ran out.'

I sat down on the seat. Dr Devereux lit his pipe and continued: 'I told Fintan to lie down. The three of them fired everything at us and finally called out, "Throw down your arms, you're surrounded!" I shouted out, "All right, I've a wounded man here!"

'I threw Fintan's revolver and Thompson gun out into the yard. I then threw out my own rifle and parabellum and two shotguns belonging to Jack Scallan and a box of cartridges. "That's all I've got, now!" I shouted.

'"Come down here, you sons of whores!' the lieutenant roared. I told Fintan to limp and walk on my left side. We came out slowly like half-dead dogs and the three remaining heroes came up to clap irons on us. I had my head on my chest, helping Fintan along. We came up to them. They relaxed. We drew abreast. The sergeant said, "Give me your wrist, Paddy." "Right," said I, and I flattened him with a box in the oesophagus. I gave the officer a head-butt in the nose and the private a clatter. All three went down.'

'Did you shoot them, doctor?' I asked reverently.

'We didn't,' he replied. 'We hanged them, collected our weapons and in one hour we were sitting down to a big feed of bacon and eggs in Murrintown. You'll have to go into the hospital. I'll get you a note for the matron and I'll send the ambulance for you on Thursday at two o'clock. You will live.'

I left the house, solemnly feeling that as I vacated those historic precincts, it would have been fitting if the 'Bold Fenian Men' or the refrain of 'Boolavogue' was performed by an orchestra with Wagnerian grandeur. Here were discussed deeds to rise the spirit.

I was driven to the hospital at half past two the following Thursday. The mother gave me two clean shirts, a book on the rebellion and an apple tart. The ambulance drew away amid bitter cries from the mother of 'The curs, the curs! A child that never did harm in his life; going to Mass and Communion.'

In the ward I was put between a bone-broken teacher and a British navy man whose whole body was in a sling –

but that did not deter him from offering impudence to those of Celtic ancestry. There was a starch of lovely badged nurses. They were of various castes and they were all on for a bit of gas. Order was kept by Sister Mary Agnes, a stern, formidable woman who put the fear of God on patients and nurses alike. At the same time, despite a cross look, she wasn't beyond a bit of a leg-pull.

I took a fancy to a lovely thing in a white uniform with the engaging combination of black hair and brown skin. Her name was Hazel Christle and she was from Church Street in Enniskillen, County Fermanagh, one of the six north-eastern counties the country was codded out of. She was greatly taken with my appearance, my injuries and chat. She was also an intellectual in her own way, despite the fact that she had not the advantage of being of our faith. She had glasses which, far from having a detractive effect, lent mirth and saucy provocation to her demeanour. She called me Nackey.

The half-saved teacher from the crags of Dingle thought he had her in the bag until I appeared. He swiftly got the message that I was number one man there. Consequently in his process of thought he embarked on a war of nerves against me. He found out that a) my nose was broken and b) I was a patient of Doctor Devereux.

Every night promptly at seven-thirty Sister M. Agnes came into the ward, got down on her knees and gave out the rosary. This was answered lustily by all, except the sailor, who donned a sailor's cap, claiming that it was the custom in his religion. The second night I was there the teacher informed me of an immodest procedure prior to every operation. It consisted of the application of soapy water to one's rear aperture through a tube held by a nurse. Fear claimed me with the panic that is nourished by ignorance. I was to be operated on the next morning. Hazel must have spotted that my mental balance was not plumb. Instantly she eyed the teacher.

'Was he on about your nose?'

I said, 'Yes, nurse,' miserably.

'Go away, you chancer,' she said to him. 'You'll be twice as good-looking when it's fixed, Nackey, don't mind him.'

The bogman made kiss sounds with his lips in time with her footfalls as she swayed her hips through the ward. She turned round and gave a swift gesture with her mouth as if to get sick. This grimace was the occasion of applause from the assembled injured. The naval officer recited a phrase of poetry with clarity of diction.

> Eleven billion pig tails, do tremble at her nod imperial –
> The which is as it should be.

I decided that he had more wit than my fellow countryman. I engaged him in lively conversation and exchanged books. I gave him Kavanagh's *Rebellion of 1798* and he gave me a book entitled *Europe's Lesser-Known Wines* which aroused my instant attention.

That evening, Hazel came in to me, to give me an injection. She made me bare my arm and when she'd finished said, ' I won't be giving you an injection there anymore, Nackey.'

I said, 'Where then, Hazel?'

'In the behind, Nackey,' she said, as bold as brass. 'Will you let me?'

I said, 'No, Hazel,' prepared to defend the exposure of that private part of the body, the contemplation, touching or sight of which for the sake of pleasure is a mortal sin. Sister M. Agnes was walking through the ward like a woman with a sack of potatoes under each arm. Hazel turned to her.

'Nackey says he'll not allow himself to be injacted in the morning, Saster.'

Sister Agnes right-wheeled at the bed. 'You give over acting the goat, my bucko. The nurse and I are sick and tired of thousands of men, and if you don't do what you're told, I'll give it to you, I tell you that.' She lumbered off, taking the ward before her. Hazel smiled in a professional attitude.

'It's not the sort of injection he told you, Nackey,' she said, pointing to the teacher. 'All it is is a little pinprick. A great big strong farmer like you wouldn't mind that.'

And off she went, tittering.

I was now assailed by fantasies. The thought of having to expose that portion of the body to one so immaculate and girlish filled me with apprehension. In fact, in plain language, the following morning I had to let down my pants and show Hazel my arse. On the other hand, as I settled down to ponder on it I must confess to spasms of pleasure which are proper only to the married state. The following day it was a vexed boy who was sucked into unconsciousness.

I came out of the operation perfect in all respects. Having shared the intimacy of my unveiling with Hazel I noticed that she became more attached to me. I sent word up to Mulcahy and MacDonagh to come and see me and I got them to bring down a pup for Hazel out of our own collie bitch, Flax. Mulcahy was very impressed with Nurse Christle and so overwhelmed with esteem was he that he presented her with a box of chocolates intended for me.

MacDonagh enquired about facilities for every need in the place, a question that supposed the satisfaction of that baser appetite which is forbidden. I ignored his query and discussed my health, which I hoped was the motivation for their visit. I also sent a note to the mother.

My dear Mother,

I am well. The tart was good. It is now all gone. Don't come up to see me until you come to collect me for I am in a ward with two men who have contagious fluorosis and I don't want you to be afflicted any more than you are.

I remain

Your loving son

Nicholas

I picked that disease out of a veterinary book. I didn't want to see the mother because she wouldn't be happy until she'd found out everyone's complaint, where they were from, and corrected Sister Agnes about the cut of the bedclothes.

Is there anyone in your family you'd prefer to have dropped dead or be gassed or hanged? I was four days in hospital making progress. I was the sole consolation of Hazel. The blight of a teacher was moved back to his reservation. He didn't leave a moment too soon. One afternoon, twenty-four hours after the delivery of my epistle to Katherine Aquinas Furlong, the door entering the ward was blacked out. Filling it, blinking and bald, was that scourge of the sensitive, Richard Smallpox MacFurlong, in the flesh, black-suited, waistcoated, with shirt but no tie. He had a hard hat in one hand and an ashplant in the other. He introduced himself with an ignorant bawl from the doorway.

'Where is the dying whelp? I can't see him.'

The dose of salts made straight for me. Hazel was present, of course. If there had been a suitcase under the bed I'd have jumped into it, even if there was a nest of rats in it.

'Here boy, eat these, they'll make you big and strong. If you don't want them, leave them there to be goddamned.'

A sugar bag was thrown on the bed. There were twelve home-made rock cakes in it with raisins in every one. He bent down over me, leering. Before he even opened his mouth he let a fart that would dust a forge.

'I knew you would end up like this, with your feck-acting around the country. There is friggin' women for you now.' He looked around the ward. 'I don't see the two hoors that are supposed to have the cholera, or was that only a gag to get rid of the auld wan? I have you taped long ago, my boy. You can't cod me, whatever about the auld heifer.'

Hazel, with her lovely black hair and tan, charming manners and deportment, was in disgust. I was mortified. Her father was a doctor and they had two cars and a summer residence in Donegal.

The uncle drained two Baby Powers of whiskey on top of what he already had. Before he left he insisted on reciting the twenty-four verses of 'Pat O'Leary' for the entire ward with ashplant gesticulations.

> My name is Pat O'Leary,
> From the borough of New Ross,
> And to see a game of football,
> I to Wexford came across.
> My brother John who came there too
> Was slow to miss his chance,
> At a wedding, wake, a funeral,
> A football match or dance.
> The whistle went, the ball was in,
> The Young Irelands ran like deers

(Wild cheers and boos from the entire ward)

But the first point was awarded
To the St John's Volunteers.

(Renewed cheers and boos from the injured)

At the close of this presentation he slapped the navy man heartily on the back with the words that his crowd were all right too, if they were taken the right way. He went away amid many ignorant guffaws. If it had been in my power to call down the widow's curse on him, I'd have put it on him.

The navy man remarked to Hazel aloud in my hearing, 'In Furlong's visitor is deposited, I fear, the loathsome effervescence of the untutored Erse. Eh, what, nurse?'

All Hazel said to me was that she was sure that there were more like him around. That bloated bag of leprotic diarrhoea did me a lot of harm. He was only half saved although he was good for a few bob now and then. The very next day, kill or cure, I left. Hazel's farewell was as warm as a wet dishcloth in a frost. One week later I went on my own to see *Caesar and Cleopatra* in the Abbey Cinema. Who did I identify in the double seats up at the back if you please? Nobody only Nurse Hazel Christle with Master Mulcahy of Mulgannon House.

12

SATISFACTION

I boast that this chapter will demonstrate upheavals inside a small area, that would do credit to the revolt of Bela Kun.

Ten days after my arrival home from hospital, I was in the yard, grinding turnips for cattle. This necessitated the manual turning of the pulper handle. A strange black car hesitated for a while and then pulled up outside the gate. A woman of substantial proportions got out. She had wind-red cheeks, bright eyes, a fleshy but agreeable body covered in a blue suit, and white frills on her bosom. She had a hat on her head full of colours and flowers. I suppose they weren't real. She looked at a picture in her hand and said to me, 'Are you over the bar?'

I replied in a not ungenerous manner that the nearest bar was Scallan's of Drinagh.

'Oh, no,' she said, 'that's not what I mean. Are you over the bar, the one who put that advertisement in the *Woman's Mind* magazine?'

I said nothing because you'd want to be careful. She pulled a cutting out of her handbag and said, 'Look here, is this you or no?'

I read the cutting and this is what it said:

'*Over the bar* is a young County Wexford farmer who is considered attractive. He has his own car, residential farm with commodious out-offices. Non-drinker. RC. Capital

£10,000. Would like to hear from nice sincere girl from 20 to 35 years of age with farm of her own, capital or dowry.'

'I surely am not "over the bar". The only car I have is a sidelace car,' I said, wondering if she took me for a fool.

'What's all this I hear?' the mother said, rubbing the potato crumbs off her hot red hands in her apron.

'Good afternoon, missus,' the strange woman said. 'Are you that boy's mother?'

'I am, thank God,' the mother replied, smiling proudly. 'What is your business?'

The well-dressed stranger in her blue two-piece suit and large Tara brooch approached the mother, not a bit put out of her stride.

'Nothing brought me all the way from Bannow only this, Mrs Furlong,' she said, diving into her handbag and producing four letters and a photograph of me in the Erin Hopes jersey alongside the whiskey puss of Charlie Fitzgerald.

'The child was a bit soft when that was taken,' the mother remarked. 'Won't you come inside a moment, Mrs . . .'

'*Miss* Mary Ann Donoghue of Hill, Bannow,' the woman said with great effect.

Now that I had a good look at her she didn't look so dusty at all and had a very attractive carriage as she walked across the yard. I kept grinding the turnips and put no more pass on the two of them. I'd enough on my mind to torment me besides them.

*

'That God may strike me down this minute, mother, if I'm telling you a word of a lie; I never wrote those letters to that woman,' I said, and I put a face of violence on myself.

'Be that as it may, Nicholas, I see the hand of someone

144

else in all this,' the mother said, looking across at the picture of her father, still draped in black crêpe after thirty years.

'It wouldn't be any harm now, Nicholas, if you paid attention to Mary Ann, for she has a warm heart and I am satisfied, your own mother, that she's made of the right stuff.'

'If you think, woman, that I am going to be sold into slavery like a convict in Siberia, you're out of your mind. What's more, she's long in the tooth,' said I with contempt.

'Hold on now a minute, Nicholas,' the mother said, smiling wisely. 'Be guided by me now. The girl has a full mouth of teeth all right and maybe she won't see thirty again but I had a few years on your father and he was well contented before God took him. Oh, don't be one bit hasty now, Nicholas, at all, for I have some news. Mary Ann has a brand new car of her own and do you know what?'

'What?' said I.

'She's calling for you next Sunday at nine o'clock to take you to Dublin to see the match. Musha, Nicholas,' the mother said, giving me the nudge with her elbow and a jaw-dropping wink, 'what great harm can come of it?'

If I could have laid hands on the cretin who concocted this predicament and sent the woman my picture, I would have opened his head with a billhook, but I allowed that I'd go anyhow for the gas.

There was nothing wrong with the day out. What would be wrong with taking the coast road to Dublin on a shining July Sunday, macaroni soup in flasks and buttered rolls, stuffed chicken, stuffed eggs and stuffed tomatoes on the strand of Brittas Bay, stretched out on a gorgeous brindle rug? Nothing. And you can add five flasks of scalding tea.

She made me bring my togs and we went in for a dip. I'm going to tell you she was one fine woman stripped, and she had a great turn of phrase. She was full of the giggles and I ate so much that the chocolates and ice cream were coming out of my ears. The match was only a display of ignorance. But after the match we went to a cinema where they served teas and dinners. There we had another feed. I didn't have to put my hand in my pocket for the whole day.

Oh yes, I noted that Sunday morning the way that Master Mulcahy and Master MacDonagh happened to be at the crest of the hill with smiles on their gobs waving goodbye to me as I set out. They weren't so goddamn funny in a fortnight's time when I was behind the wheel in Mary Ann's big car myself, waving bad luck at them. I had some right drives in it, although I had a lot to put up with again in the way of unchaste suggestion. Moses Flaherty, soils-masher and disturbance-riser, for example, came over in a sidling manner by the way of no harm. He put a blessing on me.

'God save you, Nick, asthore,' the farm Judas said. I said nothing because in the circumstances I didn't want any truck with him.

'Be led by a fool,' he said, humiliating himself, 'that wan has the weight of herself in money. If you take my advice that wan could do with a bit of a smootch. She'd be dying about you after. Tack her, Nick, tack her! It's the only dart, my poor man, and all will be yours. Take him out and make a run at her, roaring for all the world like a bull.'

The mother and Mary Ann got on like a haggard fire. I could hear the laughs and private jokes and squeals of merriment. And what do you think, but didn't Mary Ann bring the mother a pure-bred hen from Carraig-on-Bannow? All white with a red head, she was clucking and we had a great ceremony when she was put lying on a line of eggs also donated by Mary Ann. The mother put the sign of the cross on each egg with a pen while I held the bird. She then applied a liberal sprinkling of holy water

146

out of a font held by Mary Ann upon the bird and me.

'You'll have two chickens in each egg now, mother,' said I, wiping my face.

'I don't want any of your guff now, Nicholas,' the mother said. 'There's no luck on the country since the bit of religion left it.'

'True for you, Mrs Furlong,' said Mary Ann, piously but giving me the wink at the same time.

Moses Flaherty sneered that the chickens would be hatched out with eggs already laid inside the shell. 'They will in my arse. They wouldn't put wind into the common hen. Your ma wouldn't spit at them only for she got one for nothing. She'd shave a corpse for a few lousy shillings.'

I took no notice of his remarks indicative of the lower orders.

Mary Ann gave me a bottle of exotic properties. Aftershave lotion it was. It put the wits across the mother the first time she caught the stink of it on me. I used a bit of it that night in the car and I knew well by Mary Ann's signs that if I had been less of a gentleman I would not have left the occasion of sin unscathed.

I was getting on too well. The clique who started it, although I didn't know exactly who they were, weren't content to see me putting on condition and sharing Scotch eggs at hurling matches. To tell the truth, I was after getting very romantic about her too.

One night she called for me out of turn. She was very cool with the mother but I thought it was just a woman's humour. I knew she was in a mood. We went off driving, and instead of asking me what picture I'd like to go to, she drove along Wexford Quay and out to Ferrycarrig. She kept giving me the dart as she was driving along. Remarks like: 'Oh, I wouldn't be able for the hop, skip and jump' and 'Eaten bread is soon forgotten'.

147

I thought she was out of her latitude. Finally, snotty blue and sour in the face with temper, Mary Ann stopped the car underneath the castle. She produced from her purse a photo of me looking at a girl nearly in her skin with a number on her. Written across the picture was 'To Nicky's own Tootsie Wootsie with love xxxx' and the previous week's date.

I knew I was destroyed. A lot of use there'd be my shouting that I wouldn't write anything as banal as 'Tootsie Wootsie'. I knew the way it was; the begrudger had conquered again. It's a waste of time in any case to contest wits with a woman. The picture was taken at the Killurin Sports. I was standing there with my mouth open looking at the schoolgirls waiting for the hundred-yards hurdles.

She turned the car around in a shower of gravel and drove straight back to Mulgannon. There was a fever of vengeance abroad. When we got to the gate this time she kept the engine running. Not only that, but she kept on revving up.

'Go ahead in,' she said, 'your mother is lost without you.'

This final dart stung me. I got out of the car and slammed the door my living best. Off she went around the bad bend the same as if it was Fangio at the wheel.

Of course, when the oracle of Mulgannon, Katherine Aquinas Furlong, smelt that all was not well, she put on an act. She kept looking at me as if there was a want in me. She diagnosed me a flop. Chances don't always come on silver platters. Especially, as her eye-swivel indicated, to those defective in the top storey.

One morning I walked down into the town to get a licence for the gun. As I walked, my mind went back over the events in my life. There I was, humbled to pedestrian status. My reign had been of an artificial nature, since it was induced by a magazine advertisement inserted by an enemy. I pondered frequently on his or her identity. For days I thought it was the mother and gave her nothing but obstruction. Then I recalled the friendly terms they were on. Who was it? Who was it?

I used to imagine people looking at me in the street and smiling to themselves. I nurtured a hatred of whoever, with deliberate thought and diabolical cunning, had conspired against me. Was there one individual involved? Two? A group? The Erin Hopes club? Some woman scorned because I wouldn't compromise my principles? Some brain in Mulgannon? Confusion. Who was it?

I was going up to the GPO along South Main Street. I was passing by the office of the *Wexford Free Press* when a figure emerged from the door, clad in a brown overcoat, a cap and gloves. I recognised him as the far-seeing scribe, Mr Seán Gilroy. He saw me. He stopped dead in his tracks. From the corner of his mouth, eyeing me, he spoke.

'What way are you, Master Furlong?'

'I'm all right, Mr Gilroy,' I replied, stopping. We sold milk to the Gilroys in Parnell Street and it's always a good thing to be civil to those who are keeping the bit in your mouth.

'There's a great cream on the stuff you're sending us in now,' he added.

I looked him straight in the eye. 'There'd be as good a cream on everybody else's if they were as good a payer as the Gilroys,' I said with sincerity. He tightened the collar around his neck, looked furtively to the right and left, bent his head in invitation to the door and said secretly, 'Would you have a couple of minutes to spare?'

I knew by his tone of voice that he had something profound to discuss.

It was lunchtime. The *Free Press* office was dimly lit by

arrested sunlight and dust. There was a smell of newspapers and print. Mr Gilroy spoke in the same confidential tone.

'It's none of my business, but our families are old Wexford.'

He gave me a light puck on the chest – to indicate ethnic bond – and then continued. 'There was a dirty turn done on you recently.'

'What happened?' I asked.

He put his mouth up to my ear and kept looking around for interlopers. 'There was an advertisement put into a certain magazine recently. A lonely-hearts column. Am I talking?'

He paused for ten seconds.

'The party who instigated it and went to great trouble to get a photograph of the Killurin Sports was your friend Master Joseph Mulcahy of Mulgannon House.'

His hand left the lapel of my coat. He said no more but tripped swiftly out the door and pursued a fast course along the footpath, looking neither right nor left.

I walked out into the sun slowly. I looked at the big chocolate boxes in Moran's window. I saw a vision of Mulcahy's venerated mug, around which clung the incense of merchant respectability. Mulcahy! If it had been Mac-Donagh I would not have been surprised, but that other sanctimonious hoor's blocks bursting his cretin heart laughing at me . . . I couldn't believe it.

The curse of Cromwell light down on him. The big, fawning, hidden, underhanded, maniacal stag. That he may die roaring and bellowing for the priest in the dead of night, haunted by technicoloured, salacious, lewd, homo- and heterosexual orgies and visions of hell with molten eyeballs searing down a black, leathered face, ablaze with shrieks and fire.

Revenge there would have to be. I resolved not to reveal to a living soul what Mr Gilroy had told me. I decided to be the life and soul of the party if Mulcahy was in it. I would bide my time. I would plan with skill, choosing my battlefield for a revenge that would not alone equal the evil he thrust upon me but would be a classic in plan, elevation and execution. Those were the high aims I set myself, although I had to decide whether to go home for the gun and shoot Mulcahy or go to the GPO for the licence.

I returned to Mulgannon with the dead weight of the unknown lifted off my shoulders. I was subject to my parent. I was courteous to the workman, Moses Flaherty. I was the provider of gleeful anecdote to Mulcahy and MacDonagh.

Various areas of activity began to present themselves. One was the consorting of my previous intended, Nurse Hazel Christle of Wexford Hospital, to a range of functions with Master Mulcahy. The second was his lively interest in her conversion to the Roman, Catholic and Apostolic Church from her own nonconformist tradition. The importance of his task was outlined to myself and MacDonagh by Mulcahy with an intensity which paid tribute to the missionary lost in him.

MacDonagh's questions to Mulcahy did not concern the state of her soul. They concerned her approach to intimate enterprise and possibilities of a carnal nature. He posed the question of whether she would be more likely to be generous in certain facilities. Mulcahy churned with fury. It was a good job for MacDonagh that he looked harmless, or Mulcahy would have kicked the stones out of him. He responded that, whatever about immoral behaviour with a Catholic girl, what would one who had not the consolation of our religion think if one of its witnesses induced bodily knowledge? Mulcahy informed us that after going to the pictures or for a scenic drive or a gramophone recital, he spent an hour or two outside on the Hospital Road explaining the meaning of the Faith and refuting Hazel's misconceptions. He said she was an intelligent girl and a wonderful conversationalist.

'Feck it,' I said, 'I'm going home or Kate will be after me with the hounds.'

It was one o'clock in the morning when we finished arguing.

'You don't spend this long talking to Nurse Christle,' I said, indicating my ceased interest by using her polite title.

'Actually,' said Mulcahy, 'we finished discussing the matter last night at two in the morning. One goes on and on. We rarely finish before one.'

'Discussing religion?' asked MacDonagh.

Mulcahy didn't reply. I bade them good night and feck 'em for keeping me out. I had as much religion as I wanted all the next day, making haycock after haycock.

But in the making of those dusty haycocks, I saw the fall of Austerlitz. I had Mulcahy opened and exposed to me through his own big mouth.

*

I will now give an account of the circumstances and dramatis personae which, though unrelated, were woven together personally to inflict a revenge on one Joseph Mulcahy. The parish priest of Wexford was the Very Reverend George O'Brien, an ebullient man who settled affairs and the pain of the poor with gruff affection. An ailment he was not disposed to treat with balm was the desire for carnal knowledge of maidens by persons of the male occupation who had an antipathy to holy wedlock.

It is important to take note of another specimen, a queer hawk indeed. He was zealous in the curbing of that vice which is the shame of the Gael and the despoiler of the daughters of Brigid, Maeve and Dervorgilla. This, the junior curate in the parish, was a tall, sallow-complexioned ascetic named Father Senan Connick. He was the genteel director of the Women's Confraternity, the Apostolic Work and the Legion of Mary. In that last organisation were accounted the entire Mulcahy family, man, woman and boy.

It was the Venerable Connick's aim to preserve Ireland in the practices of the holy hour, novenas, pilgrimages and confraternities. By the participation in the aforementioned, one lived the Christian life and bugger all other upheavals like having no money, which was only an affliction of the mind. His aim was to restrict that biological furnace which was already engulfing the world and my native precincts in particular. He was very sweet but I did not like the looks of him. Alarm was my portion if I spotted him two hundred yards away at Roches Terrace with his eyes downcast and his soutane a-swish.

The third person to whom I would draw your attention is Miss Josephine Darcy, the senior housekeeper in the presbytery. She was a thin woman with grey hair caught in a bun. Dressed appropriately in black, she always spoke and answered calls in a reverent hush. Miss Darcy had a variety of talents. She could divine water, stop bleeding, forecast the weather, wire houses, repair plumbing, cultivate plants on concrete and manage clergymen.

It is not to be wondered that I was keenly aware of Miss Darcy's qualifications, for we – that is, the mother and I – supplied milk to Wexford. We had the contract for supplying milk to the presbytery, in which dwelt seven of the finest servants of God who ever poured cream over porridge. Mr MacDonagh senior procured this benefice for the mother on the death of my father. At the end of the family rosary it was the mother's wont to offer up a Hail Mary for Mr MacDonagh's intentions, to which I always responded with fervour. Yes, we supplied the presbytery with milk and, if the parish priest had the ear of the bishop, Miss Darcy had the ear of the parish priest, and who had the ear of Miss Darcy? Our Nicholas!

I introduce her to you since she played a significant role in the undoing of Brother Treachery Fitz Balls Mulcahy. Miss Darcy had a refined personality, so that the mere mention of anything of an unwholesome nature gave this holy soul the colic.

I resolved that the time to put manners on Mulcahy had arrived. He was escorting the indifferent Calvinist Nurse Hazel Christle thrice-weekly to events of an uplifting nature, followed by tea and biscuits in White's Hotel and then out beyond the hospital gates for non-sexual exchanges on theology. I had to make certain of this, to the extent that I had to hire Taxi Brien to drive me over the area. There I found Mulcahy with the dashboard light on, expostulating, and Nurse Christle lying back against the far window, her coat open, looking at him, waiting for it to happen, God comfort her.

The next day I hastened to the presbytery kitchen and said, 'Good morning, Miss Darcy.'

'Good morning, Master Furlong,' she said, with a hushed tone. 'This weather will bring the grass along all right. How is Mrs Furlong?'

'Game ball, Miss Darcy, but unfortunately there's trouble on her at the moment.'

'Oh,' said Miss Darcy, drawing back. 'What is it?'

I put down the three-gallon can and the measure. 'I'd tell not a living soul but yourself, Miss Darcy, because you were always good to us. Do not tell a living soul what I'm going to tell you now.'

'I most certainly will not, Master Furlong,' she promised.

'Nor,' I added in grieved tones, 'mention a word of it to my mother to cause her further distress.'

'Not a word to the decent woman, surely,' said Miss Darcy, pulling the timber chair over to the table and sitting down in anticipation of the shock to be unleashed upon her soul.

'The mother's niece,' I said. 'Seventeen. Great hopes of the veil. Gone to Birmingham! A commercial traveller who is a married man.'

Miss Darcy slumped forward in her chair and placed her hand upon her breast. She said nothing for surely one minute, but spent that period contemplating the large, shiny bread-knife. She arose and put her hand on my shoulder.

'I'll get you a cup of tea and cake. It's a queer world, surely. Oh, God help us. No safety for man, woman, boy or girl.'

We sat there chatting solemnly. Miss Darcy said the world was gone to sin and wickedness.

'The world is right, Miss Darcy, and where would you leave our little town?'

'Oh, that's the question, Master Furlong,' she said, 'that's the question.'

'That is the question,' I said, rising up in my wrath, 'and God between us and all hurt and harm, there are queer things going on. Three unfortunate girls, not mentioning names – two from this parish – left on the mailboat last Wednesday night.'

Miss Darcy brought her white knuckles to her mouth.

'And I don't care what anyone says, now, it's not always the men's fault, Miss Darcy.'

She smiled and looked around the kitchen. 'Who are you telling, Master Furlong? There are girls today who don't know what rope is holding the mast.'

'I'm afraid . . . ' I said, 'I'm afraid . . . '

'What are you afraid of?' asked Miss Darcy in alarm.

'I'm afraid there may be more trouble on the way.'

'God bless us, what?'

'I know for a fact, Miss Darcy, of a sad case of a nurse in the County Hospital who is anti-Catholic.'

'A . . . ' The word died on Miss Darcy's lips.

I nodded deeply twice and carried on. 'She has the son of one of the most respectable and charitable Catholic families in all Wexford out every second night. And he spends the night with her in a car on the Hospital Road, an uncle a priest, may God preserve him from all temptation, Miss Darcy.'

*

I am indebted to the following sources for information without which it would have been impossible to piece together this narrative, viz. Mrs Mulcahy's maid, Miss Darcy; MacDonagh; Nurse Shivaun O'Toole, an enemy of Nurse Christle; and the Rev Miles Byrne CC, a very good man who showed me how to make money out of grassland and get grants for improvements.

The film to which Mulcahy brought the bird was entitled *The Razor's Edge* and the chief character was Tyrone Power, a Waterford man now deceased, RIP. Afterwards, at 11.15 PM, they glided in the Mulcahy family car toward the hospital road. This road was well illuminated up to the main hospital entrance. However, on passing the entrance, one was engulfed in blackness. Master Mulcahy drove his car beyond the bright lights and embraced satanic darkness.

A lively conversation ensued to the satisfaction of both, when at 1.15 AM a small car with the dims on drew up in front of them. A dark figure approached them from the small car. There was a chilling series of knocks on the window of the Mulcahy vehicle.

Mulcahy lowered the window and peered out into the

night. The apparition which crystallised was the Savonarolic image of the Reverend Senan Connick CC. He coughed, and addressed the occupants of the smoke-filled car in soft soprano.

'We have received complaints about some of the conduct on this road.'

*

Let us now consider Mulcahy's position. Of what avail was it, pray, to state they were only talking? None. One could shout a three-hour debate in a thousand well-lighted venues in the town. Of what avail to accuse his reverence of an unwarranted intrusion into privacy, followed by the suggestion that he be gone at once? None, for this would have displayed a lack of unity and filial devotion to a minister of the Church before a nonconformist on the verge of conversion. Of what avail to suggest that missionary effort was being mounted upon Nurse Christle by the courteous driver? None, unless the desired effect was to reduce the tormented Aaronite to shrieks of disbelief.

On the morrow, visits were paid in genteel, helpful fashion by the Rev Senan Connick CC to a) the matron of the hospital, Mother Mary Agnes and b) the Mulcahy residence, Mulgannon House.

In her resignation speech to the matron, Nurse Christle sublimated the poisonous fury in her breast into polite reasoning. She could not reconcile her ambition to study in these parts with the situation obtaining. She questioned the practice of an unmarried celibate engaging in spying throughout the dark hours. It was regrettable that this was considered acceptable. She suggested that the Rev Senan Connick could himself be considered a sensual peril. In any case she was immediately taking up a position in the County Fermanagh General Hospital.

The result of the helpful, genteel visit by the Rev Senan Connick to Mulgannon House was the patriarchal rage of Mr Mulcahy and Mrs Mulcahy. Master Mulcahy was so confused by the manner of the attack on all fronts that he listened in wide-eyed and open-mouthed silence. He was close to emulating a Soviet-trial tradition of confessing to defects he never had. Thus there was staged the spectacle of an honest, well-behaved, mannered, chaste boy demonstrated before his parents to be a profligate spendthrift, family-car abuser, fornicator, anticleric, pugilist and dunce. It was a classical and historic revenge which fitted the iniquity of his own deed.

Reports of the event seeped out around Mulgannon. MacDonagh first informed me that Father Connick discovered Mulcahy in an exposed state of excitement, undressed, and that as a result he, Father Connick, had to be sent to the Mental. That was only wishful thinking from MacDonagh. The immediate result was that Mulcahy was detailed to work of a menial nature so that the edge might be taken off him. He was sent up to us for a trailer-load of dung for the Mulgannon House garden. He was on his own loading it. The mother suggested that I give Mr Mulcahy a helping hand. I said that I had no objection to giving Mr Mulcahy a helping hand but that I did not wish to be with someone possessed of a record for immorality.

'How the hell could he get out of it?' the mother said, as if contemplating some dark secret.

That night I lay wide awake in bed, thinking about the whole issue. I was not happy after all. I had to allow that there was a touch of the monster in me.

13

THE MONAGEER HAMLET

The mother was no daw.

One day I was in the kitchen, reading the riddles in *Ireland's Own*. The mother was knitting a red gansey. She had a thoughtful expression on her face and was so busily engaged in knitting that she hadn't time to blow her nose. Every now and again she stripped her teeth and snuffled a hawl vigorously. She stopped.

'How old are you now, hon?' she asked.

The alarm went off in my head. 'I'm nearly twenty,' I said, adopting a defensive attitude. The mother got up.

'What are you but a big soft child still?' the mother sighed, 'but all the same, you're shaving.' She threw me a sudden look under the bright spectacles. 'I never gave you wrong advice, Nicholas, and I want you to listen very carefully to all that I have to say. Gold locks, fancy words and the come-hither look never put anything on a man's plate or a garment on his back. I do not want you to throw yourself away.'

I hadn't being doing anything out of the way. Sure, I was at a few dances with the boys and talent competitions and matches, but that was all. 'You must think I'm a right gawk,' I said. 'All I'm having is a bit of gas, going around.'

'Oh, Nicholas,' the mother said, 'in this world the time for gas is very short indeed. Faith, we'd all be fond of gas if it came to that. Damn the much gas I ever got. I want you to steady yourself. You ought to be on the lookout for a good sensible match, a girl with a respectable background, a farm of land to her name, and better again if she had a few shillings at her back.'

'And where does romance come in, Mother, or do you know anything about love?' I asked with my temper mounting.

'Ah, child,' she said with that sad sweet smile of hers, 'you can have every bit as much love and romance with a girl who has money as with a girl who has none. Are you going to tell your mother how to suck eggs? There's a girl not two miles from here, Nicholas, and if you have any brains you'll go and dance attendance on her.'

'Who's that?' I rapped out.

'Nollaig Sinnott,' the mother delivered triumphantly.

I'd no fault on the girl at all, only she had an impudent face, knew everything and said that going to a dance on bicycles was common. She was from Rathaspeck, around the block from us, still on the Mulgannon plateau though not of our immediate community. She was convent-educated and she could paint pictures. Her daddy had a huge contract for pigs in the bacon factory as well as milk and he was on the county committee of agriculture. He often had his name in the papers for attacking officials. The mother announced that he was elected every year for one thing only and that was to raise dirt. The uncle Dick said he was only a fountain-pen farmer.

It was not Mr Sinnott who was the dirt-riser at all, but Mrs Sinnott. I did not like Mrs Sinnott. I would have been across the fields after Nollaig years before if it wasn't for her mother's scaldy spout. She didn't look down on me at all. She ignored me as if I were not of the same species as the Sinnotts. And what were they only farmers, the same as ourselves? Maybe they had a few more shillings in the bank but what does that signify? So had Al Capone.

Mrs Sinnott had the whole issue summed up for her offspring. Her principles were that the pen, the stick of chalk, the breviary or the forceps were a hell of a lot lighter than a four-tagged fork with beet or dung. And what would I bring on a daughter of hers if God-given affection were nourished? Enlightenment? Cultured repartee? Security and travel abroad? The vision that crossed her mind in my regard would be that of her child crossing the yard in Mulgannon with two buckets of slops, followed by hungry sows chawing the knickers off her.

Nollaig was inoffensively plump, with a figure which insinuated disregard of virtue. She was all gone on the theatre and was secretary of the Rathaspeck Dramatic Society, which put on plays regularly by authors of the Irish tradition. Nor, may I add, were the European or North American masters neglected. I decided – after giving the matter some thought and to pacify the mother – to go across to Nollaig's house and ask her if she'd take my name to join the dramatic society. To tell the truth, I always wanted to be an actor.

Nollaig's daddy met me at the gate and tipped his hat back on his head, looking for conversation. I told him a joke I'd heard down the town. Hearty laughter from Mr Sinnott. Next at the door peering out was the banshee Sinnott, his wife, enquiring no doubt what I, the scrapings of hell, was doing there. Mr Sinnott told her I was going to be an actor and to send Nollaig out.

'Come in,' said Mrs Sinnott. 'She's drying her hair.'

I was put into the kitchen, which had a big floor covered with red tiles.

At the back of the door was nailed a wide sprig of blessed palm. Near the window was the picture of St Patrick driving the snakes out of Ireland into the sea, thus saving the Gael from this reptilian peril.

Enter Nollaig Sinnott with a steaming hot face and black streams of wet hair being vigorously rubbed. She looked like a boiled plum pudding. 'Very well then, Nicholas Furlong,' Nollaig said, 'but it's hard work and you'll have to do something about your voice.'

The latter oration was necessitated by the fact that the play they were doing was *Hamlet* by William Shakespeare, as if they couldn't pick one about Ireland. Here, by the laws of coincidence, I was on to a winner. I might not have been the brightest in the parish but if there was one gentleman I knew off by heart it was Hamlet, Prince of Denmark, and I'll tell you why.

The mother sent me to school in Wexford town, to the Christian Brothers. One autumn day we got a new teacher because we had advanced to sixth class. His name was Brother Barragry. He was very artistic and used to play the fiddle at concerts. A bony man, with grey hair and glasses, he spent some time trying to discover every pupil's bent. *Tales from Shakespeare* was on the course, but Brother Barragry was mad on *Hamlet*. One day, I was asked by the brother to stand up and read out a piece of that play. I started at the speech which is world-famous.

'To be or not to be, that is the quesken.'

The manner of this delivery seemed to have a hypnotic effect on Brother Barragry for he looked at me very queerly and he asked me to start off again, which I did. He then addressed me in quiet tones. He said that he had taught in Cabra, Cork, Belfast, Clonmel, Sydney and Sierra Leone but that he had never heard the like of it before. He assured me in what intuition advised me was a menacing manner that before he (Brother Barragry) was twelve months older, I (Nicholas Furlong) would learn a new language: English. I decided that it would be a safe course to cooperate. That is how I got to know *Hamlet*.

I entered the Rathaspeck Dramatic Society with no sense of inferiority – nay, rather had I high claims upon doing that character who had very bad luck in his family life. He wasn't the mutt he was made out to be by his uncle, who unlawfully possessed his mother with 'things rank and gross in nature'.

The mother was beside herself with joy and I gave her an account every night of the way we read out the play. Then the moment came when the selection committee gave the parts out. The part of Hamlet was given to a gentleman named Peadar Sugrue. This mastitis Einstein was one of the latest gentry in the country. He was a bachelor of agricultural science in Johnstown Castle, which houses Ireland's soils-research division.

A soil researcher, that's what he was, and there was a whole heap of them down there from all over Ireland. They had the Wexford women's heads turned with their motor cars, security, brains and government jobs. You'd see them come into a dance hall and the immediate impact was the arrested attention of the best women in the place. I hadn't put any pass on this gentleman, beyond reflecting that, from his appearance, he couldn't be trusted. Nor did I ever think that he had the wildest hope in hell of assaulting the ears of the sensitive with major quotations from the Bard of Avon upon the timber stage.

I was given the part of the gravedigger.

*

'They are after doing the child out of his part and giving it to the stranger. The stranger to get on in Wexford and the emigrant ship for the native son. They come in on top of us with empty suitcases and the arse out of their trousers and in twelve months they're all in all with everyone, and when they leave – a big feed and a wallet of notes. He'll have to be got rid of,' the mother issued forth to the Sacred Heart picture in the kitchen. 'I'll do a novena to St Anthony.'

As sure as God is my judge, she did the novena, and one bare week before we were billed and posted to appear in St Catherine's Hall, Murrintown, Sugrue went down in a heap at his monumental plant pathology, was rushed to hospital and operated on for appendicitis.

> Unhousel'd, disappointed, unanel'd,
> No reckoning made, but sent to his account
> With all his imperfections on his head:
> O, horrible! O, horrible! most horrible!

'God grant us no greater loss' was my prayer when I heard the news. Of course Nollaig was distraught.

'Whom shall we approach?' she cried to the cast.

'Fret no longer, Nollaig,' I boldly replied. 'My pulse as yours doth temperately keep time and/Moves as beautiful music:/It is not madness I have utter'd:/Bring me to the test . . . '

Heads turned. Mouths opened. Conversation ceased. That was the queer old slap in the snot for Nollaig and the rest who had me down for a turnip-snagger. There was new respect among the thespians.

I got the part, and not alone that, but I was the soothing escort of Nollaig Sinnott, whose attitude changed from tolerance to infatuation. She told Father O'Brien and her mother that I looked distinguished.

Mrs Katherine Aquinas Furlong of Mulgannon, mother of the leading actor, got a perm with a blue rinse for the opening night in Murrintown Hall. Because of that relationship to the leading actor, much was made of her. Her appearance and reception cut the ground from under the begrudging sector. The only bags made of the night happened when I dispatched Polonius. The uncle, bloated with booze and ignorance, wheezed from the back of the hall, 'Good enough for the aul' fecker; come on the Hopes!'

By a fortunate chance, a distinguished critic, Mr Alois de Barra, who often adjudicated at drama festivals, was present with Father George O'Brien, our parish priest, and Canon Bazely of the Church Protestant and reformed. Mr de Barra may have come to scoff, but he remained to pray. He submitted a criticism to the three County Wexford papers which I have much pleasure in quoting.

The following extract is from the *Wexford Free Press*.

> '*Les trops délicats*' were possibly absent from St Catherine's Hall, Murrintown on Tuesday night. They were not mourned. This offering was immediate, contemporary, authentic. Though some roles were penalised by physical incongruity, yawning multitudes were covered by brash Teutonic diction delivered with sincerity that burned. In retrospect, production is not, cannot, be chastised in view of certain architectural hazard. The play's the thing.
>
> Shakespeare was untroubled by vulgar things (the same cannot be said for Yeats). His entire work was an attempt to achieve a complete human image, which to him was an image of men, body and soul, revealed in action. Granted these allegiances, to what other metaphor could Shakespeare turn for his need?
>
> The Murrintown *Hamlet* is virgin. What impertinence to suggest that there is a Shakespeare

mode, a tone, a pronunciation! Does the absence of
these mythical qualities invalidate a performance in
Moscow, Greenwich, in Heidelberg, or – dare I say
– Murrintown?

Mr de Barra concluded with words of encouragement for the
development of a local 'indigenous' theatrical tradition
without respect or fear for the cant of vociferous pseudo-
sophisticates. 'The true sophisticate,' he added, 'is still to be
found moulding the soil of Ireland.'

Nollaig entered us for the All-Ireland Rural Drama
Competition. The first heat of this competition was in
Monageer Hall, a small but important village in the middle
of the county. Despite the distance, everyone in Mulgannon
got tickets, and to make the affair convenient, a bus was
hired to convey friends and enemies alike up to Monageer.
Mulcahy and MacDonagh travelled as well. I had stopped
knocking around with them while I was engaged in theatrical
expression. During this period, I often considered the vacancy
of their minds, the lack of depth in their remarks, Mac-
Donagh's lewd cackle and the entrepreneurial lack in
Mulcahy's thought.

The Johnstown Castle man had recovered by this time
too and we decided to give him the part of the gravedigger.
But there was a bitter look about him and being the
gravedigger didn't suit him one bit. No, he wanted to be the
fairy on the Christmas tree, with a sparking dandelion in his
mouth. He drove Mr and Mrs Sinnott up in his hire-purchase
car, along with the props and Nollaig.

The play went off like a bomb in Monageer. There was
an overflow attendance, as expected. The first row of seats,
which were attached to each other, bore upon them the
distinguished frames of the Roman Catholic dean of the

diocese of Ferns, the Church of Ireland rector of Coolstuff, the Methodist minister in Gorey, the Presbyterian minister in Enniscorthy, the adjudicator with his desk, the sergeant of the guards, the national school principal, the dispensary doctor and Mrs Flynn, the mother roasting with grandeur, Mr and Mrs Sinnott of Whiterock, the uncle Dick and the secretary of the Farmers' Union.

Who is there who has trod across the timber stage and does not thrill to communication between actor and audience? I was in my element and the plain people could make out everything I said. The part of Ophelia was played by Peggy Codd from Coolballow, who was as graceful as a wheelbarrow. I had hoped that Nollaig might play the part and allow me some chance of character-adjustment in a romantic manner, but Nollaig took the part of the Queen. She wasn't bad either, except that she fell dead each night like a collapsed horse. Timing was not her forte – but enough of that.

We came to the burying of Ophelia. You might know the story of the play, because it is famous. When Ophelia is in the grave, being buried as a suicide under a moral cloud, the brother, Laertes, turns up and is overcome by grief. He begs to be buried alive with his sister. 'Now pile your dust upon the quick and dead,' he declaims in a very sad speech.

At that very moment, Hamlet, played by me, is supposed to spring from the wings, where he is concealed for a minute or two, and roar in anguish:

> What is he whose grief
> Bears such an emphasis? Whose phrase of sorrow
> Conjures the wandering stars and makes
> > them stand
> Like wonder wounded hearers? This is I,
> Hamlet, the Dane.

167

I was in love with Ophelia, you see, and at this point I was to buck-leap into the mound in centre stage which represented the grave. My self-confidence soared but I had reckoned without one unadulterated savage. The craven melt from the western bogs pushed his shovel between my legs as I raced and leaped. I have a vision of the audience rushing forward in rowed formation to swallow me – Roman collars, adjudicator's glasses, women and the shiny pillar of Dick Furlong's head as with raised arms he roared in fright. I hurtled at full speed into them, bringing the first two rows of seats with me. There was a spectacle of crashing chaos, tumult and stampede.

When civilisation was restored, Nollaig Sinnott turned on me, screaming with carnivorous tongue. The last I saw of her was going off with the malignant Sugrue, arm in arm, and fire burning in her eyes amid the wreckage of our All-Ireland hopes.

I was down the field once more.

But the mother was proud as punch of me and she told me not to bother my head crying over the loss of that three-quarter.

'The dog, Nicholas,' the mother said, 'does not go into mourning when the jackass dies. There's plenty of fish to be caught in the sea yet.'

The woman was right. I gave up the idea of hanging myself in the grove. The person who would deceive the mother would want to be up at an early hour in the morning.

14

PERIL

This chapter is about a romance which was not of a personal-involvement nature. It was a romance, however, upon which I was compelled to keep a most sharpened eye.

It was the merry month of May and there was a yellow outrage of furze blossom in Mulgannon. There was also an epidemic of cows running in excitement on fresh grass and breaking out of their fields. One Wednesday evening, when the mother got in the cows for milking, Lar Roche was gone. She was a silky brown shorthorn. She was called Lar Roche because we bought her off Lar Roche for thirty-two pounds and a quid for luck. She was a right milker.

'Off with you now, Nicholas, like a ton of bricks,' the mother said, 'and bring back Lar Roche before she gets torn to the gizzard on the briars.'

In order to facilitate my legs, I made for Moran's big rock and took in the panorama which stretched before me, from the Blackwater lightship to the Saltee Islands. I brought my vision down to bear on the small fields and hedges. When I beamed across to Mulgannon, an unusual tableau appeared on the dusty road. There was Lar Roche, swishing her long brown tail in temper and marching smartly back towards Mulgannon. Behind her, wheeling a bicycle, was a uniformed member of the Garda Siochána of Ireland. He was wheeling the bike with his left hand, and every now and then he rose his right hand over Lar Roche and shouted, 'How! How!'

Guards are parties I don't like tangling with. The first scent that I smelt was trouble. Flight was the impulse I acted on at once.

I told the mother there was a guard coming up the road with Lar Roche. The mother's jaw dropped. The vision of another sledgehammer of unhappy fortune flooded her mind.

'Oh, mild and sweet Jesus,' the mother exclaimed, 'she has torn up Stafford's garden by the roots.' She turned on me. 'You're a good thing. You're not fit to fence a hen, bringing the blasted peelers down on top of me.' Her low psychiatric state at this time was responsible for the perilous days through which I was destined to pass.

'God save the good woman,' said the loud Connemara voice that followed Lar Roche into the yard.

'Kindly,' the mother said, and then in grand surprise, 'My goodness, look at our little cow; wherever have you been?'

'Nowhere at all, my good woman; the grand little cow was nowhere at all – you may rest your mind easy on that point.'

The custodian of the peace rested his bike against the gate, removed a large ledger from the back carrier, lifted his cap above his sweat and approached the Seat of Wisdom. It was plain to be seen that he was, at the end of his days, keeping the bright side out. He had a trim enough figure, due, no doubt, to the eschewing of those factors which militate against a healthy body and mind. He had a full face, a greying sandy muss, loose teeth and a gimlet eye.

'I was taking the statistics, you see, down the road – 'tis the time for it, you know – and, by the hokey, down came her ladyship, I was informed it was none other than your good self who owned her and, since I was coming here in any event on a call, I took the liberty of bringing her back, a grand sweet little lady she is too.'

This rigmarole was issued in a loud voice in the accents I have indicated without the deliverer once drawing breath. The mother opened up like a tropical flower. The statistics! That's what it was then. And since we were the last house on the road, he must have been in the rest of the houses, noting down their acreages and stock and being told every stir about us. The advantage we had was that the mother could read what the rest claimed they had. The reason for this fact-finding excursion has ever been obscure to me, but no less obscure than the facts are to the government when the returns are sent back.

In relief the mother invited the guard to accept hospitality. She gathered herself importantly over the table and watched as two full rounds of home-made brown bread and butter were washed down the open throat of the visitor by a pint of new milk, without the slightest difficulty.

'I'm going to tell you this now, ma'am,' the guard said, "tis the schweetest bread and the schweetest milk that I ever downed and I've been stationed in every county in Ireland. A fact.'

'Oh, ho, ho, get away out of that with you now,' said the mother, all risen up in herself and waving a limp hand towards him like a young one.

"Tis no wonder the boy has the red neck on him like a bull,' he added. 'Has he a mind for the work or the books?'

'Nicholas is very biddable, I must say,' the mother said.

'Sound, sound,' said the guard. 'Now ma'am, schtock. Cows?'

The mother now adopted a new routine and lowered her voice to a whisper.

'Fourteen, Sergeant . . . '

'Brodar is my name, ma'am, Garda Brodar. Eh boy, did you read about the Brodar fellow that laced King Brian Boru in Clontarf, when he was praying instead of fighting? I'm one of them.'

The imparting of this valuable information caused him to turn around to the mother and laugh with robust and infectious vigour. The mother also laughed and remarked that Mrs Brodar had a very good-humoured husband. This civil remark also drew forth a renewed jawful of laughter, which ceased with abruptness, as if a wand had been whipped across his face. Deadly serious, he said, 'But sure, Mrs Furlong dear, I'm not married at all at all.'

'My goodness gracious, Guard Brodar,' the mother said, searching him for some physical defect, 'what happened to you and the world full of women, now?'

'The world is full of thackeens and schtrollers, woman dear, but not sensible girls with sensible notions,' Guard Brodar said – and here I may point out a phonetic peculiarity which I refuse to spell out any longer. Whenever the guard uttered a word beginning with 's' and followed by 't', 'p', 'k', 'l' or 'q', he added the letters 'ch' after the 's'. Thus 'speak' became 'schpeak' and 'study' became 'schtudy'. This peculiarity is indicative of Firbolg ancestry, a tribe domiciled on the western seaboard which retreated underground before the civilising influences of the Celt.

'Cattle under two years of age, excluding in-calf heifers?'
'Twelve.'
'Suck calves?'
'Five. I'd have had six, only the cursed – the beast died from overfeeding,' the mother said, not wishing to bring the word 'scour' before Guard Brodar at the table.
'Losses, losses, losses. Declare to God, if the farmer could keep alive what's born into the place itself, he'd be well off,'

remarked Guard Brodar, scribbling with the sucked top of a pencil.

'It went instead of something else, I always say, Guard Brodar,' remarked the mother. 'Better that than a human Christian.'

The guard threw down his pencil. 'Oftentimes you'd wonder, ma'am.'

'Oh, indeed,' responded the mother enigmatically.

'Sows?'

'Two.'

'How many pigs do you fatten?'

'Twelve, twice a year.'

The collector of statistics looked up as if to say that if he had two sows, he'd have thirty-six fatteners. 'Luck plays a large part in the pig' was the statement he settled for.

'Acreage of entire farm?'

'Ninety-five acres,' whispered the mother.

'Yerra, it's a ranch you have, Mrs Furlong,' the guard observed.

'Oh, now, Mr Brodar,' said the mother, adopting the lay title of respect, 'I'm going to tell you we're put to the pin of our collar.'

'The pin of your collar? You're having me on,' stated the officer of the law with bulging eyes.

'I am not, Mr Brodar – losses and costs, losses and costs.'

'My brother Peter Paul has twenty-nine acres in west Galway, ten cows, twenty sheep, eight sows and he fattens fifty. There's not a race meeting that doesn't see him, nor a football match. The family's reared. One in the guards, one in the States, one married into a neighbour's place and the daughter in the civil service and he's as light as a spring lamb, up in the morning at half five there, as healthy as a trout and he has the little motor car and trailer as well and brings vegetables into Galway. I wish I'd a quarter of his wad.'

The antennae of the mother's mind absorbed this barrage of information but correlated it only with visible effort. 'How does he do it, Mr Brodar, in the world at all?'

The guard laughed a non-funny ha-ha as a gesture to the mother's simplicity. He said nothing but set up the following motion in mime. With his forefinger he first tapped the muscles in his arm and then the side of his head above his right ear slowly and lightly. He had indicated the springs of wealth possessed by his Herculean brother which he shared by blood connection. Those gestures indicated the physical ability of Brodar, Peter Paul, to put into effect his industrious impulses, and secondly, the abundance of brains roofed by his brother's skull. It was on the tip of my tongue to ask him if there was any chance of getting a foal out of his brother Peter Paul. The mother, however, was deeply moved. Only myself could appreciate the emotion. She allowed herself a gesture which escaped her only at moments of profound impact. She slowly closed the lid of her left eye until it was only a slit.

'Now, ma'am, there are other questions I want to ask, but I have an important engagement, so I will postpone our talk until tomorrow, please God.'

'Oh, Mr Brodar, I wouldn't dream of asking you to come up the steep hill of Mulgannon again for love or money. I'll go down to the barracks; Nicholas will drive me down,' the mother thought fit to say.

'Not a word of it, ma'am. I love the country and farming and I have other investigations to conclude here with another party, so mum's the word. I'm well fit and used to travelling over hills twice as steep and long. Don't talk to me about hills and rocks, oh no, by the hokey.'

It was at this stage that I made the mistake of making a contribution – not that there was anything wrong with that, but it produced a response from the visitor. 'All the same, Guard, farm life is very hard. There is very little money to be got for all the hard work. There is a whole lot more money to be made out of being a civil servant,' I said, elevating him.

For the moment he said nothing. He went to the door and studied the vista with the joy of the visionary. He looked across the Irish Sea, Tuskar, the harbour waters. There was a smile on his face as he adopted the traditional stance of thumb in breast pocket. He side-nodded his head and, still gazing, uttered the following lines to the distant sea:

> Give fools their gold and knaves their power.
> Let fortune's bubbles rise and fall,
> Who sows a field or trains a flower,
> Or plants a tree is more than all.

'Goodbye now, Mrs Furlong, thank you kindly for your lovely tea and may God bless you all,' concluded Guard Brodar in benediction. As he cycled down the dusty road out of sight, the mother heaved a sigh.

'That's the most light-hearted man that's been in this place, Nicholas, for twenty years. It would do your heart good, and by my song, there's a bit of the scholar attached to him too,' said the mother, all gay in herself.

I did not like the turn of events.

I was not present on the next occasion the guard arrived to conclude his investigations, for after dinner the mother sent me down to the forge on the Crescent Quay to have the young horse shod. She informed me when I returned that Guard Brodar had been present and her interrogation was over, thanks be to God, giving the impression that she was indifferent to his absence for the next twenty-four months.

Moses Flaherty, farmworker, informed me however that ye arm of ye law arrived in the yard whistling 'The Lark in the Clear Air' at 2.30 PM and left whistling 'The Coolin' at 5.30 PM, prior to which he had walked the fields behind the house with the mother and inspected the outhouses. He had not scaled dizzy heights in Mosie Flaherty's affection. Mosie told me he was an impudent bugger. On the occasion he crossed the yard with the mother, he, Moses Flaherty, doused a Woodbine and emitted a smoker's cough to clear his lungs. Without looking at him, the gendarme passed the remark out loud, 'A dry cough is the trumpeter of death.'

I noticed, from that day on, recurring incidents. The mother insisted on attending the novena devotions every Sunday night in Bride Street church and the holy hour every first Friday. I used to go to pacify the mother because she said that if we didn't, God knows what bad luck might fall on the place. Every time we entered the church I found Guard Brodar either two seats in front of us or two seats behind us with a rosary beads over his clenched fist and his mouth going in prayer like a cement mixer. There was nothing outlandish in that, you might say. Ah no, nothing at all, except that he was in digs in George's Street, which is at the other end of the town and has two churches of its own, Rowe Street and the Friary.

One Sunday afternoon I was stuck for cash when in town with Mulcahy and MacDonagh. Mulcahy agreed to drive me back up to Mulgannon. When I walked into the kitchen of my house I found the mother, all flustered, dusting pictures on the wall, and Guard Brodar, with his coat on the back of the door, was sitting over the fire, mouth-reading a book with intent.

'Would you give us the loan of ten bob?' I said.

'Certainly, Nicholas,' the mother said.

'One minute now, Katherine,' Guard Brodar said, whipping his hand into his pocket and providing fifteen shillings. He slapped it into my hand and closed my fingers over it with his fist. I was confused and turned to the mother, who smiled encouragement at me with a contented expression.

'Go on now, boy, you're young,' Guard Brodar said, 'and remember the old saying, "Keep your mouth and your purse close".'

I told the boys that there was a guard up visiting the farm. To that, Mulcahy passed a remark so casual that it was sinister.

'You should be getting used to him by now,' he said.

I should be getting used to him by now! I should be getting used to him by now! The clammy cold hand of fear placed itself upon me. Imagination, suspicion and spasmodic disbelief set up a sandstorm of fright, the propriety of which was confirmed, degree by degree.

He would arrive unannounced, take a slash-hook and go down to the rocky field to cut furze bushes. He'd bring matches to set bushes on fire, and soon smoke and flame would blot the world out of sight of Mulgannon.

'The only way to clean the land, Katherine,' he told the mother as my stomach turned to a vomit. 'Katherine', no less. Another day there was a conspiracy to get me out of the way. I was sent to Mythen's of Screen, nine miles away, for one lousy bag of Kerrs Pinks seed potatoes, months after they should have been sown!

When I returned, I intruded in my own home upon an intimate tableau. The mother had taken out of the bedroom a big gramophone with an amplifying horn on it, that hadn't seen the light of day since the Eucharistic Congress. When

177

I entered, Benjamin was there. Oh yes, Benjamin – did I not mention that before? Benjamin after Disraeli, the empire-builder, no doubt: Benjamin Mary Brodar.

The mother – or if you prefer, Katherine – and Benjamin were listening to a recording of John McCormack singing with piano accompaniment 'My Mary of the Curling Hair', the appreciation of which they acknowledged with smiles. I was forbidden by an uplifted police hand from opening my mouth. A wink followed and the good guard reached down for the pièce de résistance. He pulled a new record out of its cover and announced, with yellow teeth stripped in a cultured smile, '"The Moon Hath Raised Her Lamp Above" from *The Lily of Killarney* sung by the Emerald Isle Quartet.'

I withdrew to the calf-house to contemplate as the clear notes in the kitchen of:

> The moon hath raised her lamp above
> To light the way to thee my love,
> To light the way
> To thee my love.

were distorted by the distance to a weird metallic beep.

*

I was prepared to tolerate this crucifixion with the help of God, and might well have done, were it not for one slip. I'm not very handy. While there's nothing wrong with me mentally, my head is not able to coordinate my hand movements. The mother had to tie my bootlaces and necktie until I was twelve. I am very sensitive on the point. I resent this cross I was given to bear.

One day, I brought in a horse-load of sally branches to

the yard. I had two ropes across the load from behind, tied around the shafts in a bow-knot. By the time I got in, they were loose and the load was falling around everywhere. Benjamin Brodar was in the yard. He took one look at the load, came across and addressed me in sneered tones. 'Come out of the way, you two ends of an eejit.'

I felt as if I had got a belt of a cow's tail saturated with slop. Bottled rage nearly blew my fingernails off with the fuse of his impudence, the hairy, concupiscent herm-aphrodite.

He opened the rope off the shaft, made a loop on the rope high up on the load, put the end of the rope through the loop, brought it down around the shaft, gave one mighty heave and tightened the load so that a fly couldn't crawl between the branches.

'Mr Brodar will teach you a whole lot of ways to do things, Nicholas,' the mother said helpfully.

'I will,' rejoined the gendarme, 'if he's inclined to learn.'

But Nicholas was finished with the gendarme, because Nicholas does not take kindly to being underestimated or called the two ends of an eejit.

I considered there and then the upshot of the position obtaining. Here was a member of the forces of the law close to retirement. What better place to lay his head for the rest of his days than a snug farm with a respectable woman? Fine scenery, fresh air, milk, meat and eggs. He'd live forever. All very simple, cut and dried. He was after the bit of land.

The mother spotted advantages in this man. He was strong. He had a good head and a broad back. He wouldn't be the sort to lash money around, for at the entrance to the functions to which he brought her – like the apostolic work exhibition, the pilgrimage to Lady's Island, the pioneer rally, the Redmond Park, the museum in Dublin, holy hours,

179

funerals and wakes – there was no admission fee. Instead of insulting the mother, this sent her off in paeans of pleasure. A man was found to frequent respectable pastimes without spending a tosser. He was coming into a pension on which he could live, and she could give Moses Flaherty the high road.

She had mentioned ninety-five acres. Of those ninety-five acres – three times that with which Benjamin Mary Brodar's brother had made a fortune in Connemara – twenty-five were rock, furze bush and scenery. What better man to put into the knocks and fox covers, to roll the stones and stub the bushes? *He* bury the mother? The mother would have him wrecked inside three years, but by then she'd have ninety-five acres of land.

The question to be considered, however, was not the farm, Benjamin Brodar, the mother, the pension or romance. If a permanent liaison was arranged, the question was, whither Nicholas?

'He'll give you the road,' Mosie Flaherty said, 'but you don't give a fiddler's shite, you're young. Maybe you'd tack New York or Birmingham or out foreign in Borneo – what do you care?'

*

The uncle Dick came up to the Mulgannon road. He had taken the short cut right across the land from Poulbrean to avoid the mother. He saw me going out with the cows and came after me, blue in the face with exertion and puffing. Half-crying, aghast at the situation unfolded to him in a public house by Sergeant O'Leary, he came upon me.

'I knew she was insane, I always knew it; I warned your father not to take her, but no – what was I only the family

180

clown? The whole world laughing at us and she bringing that bull's vomit in on the floor, the farm my father and his father before him sweated blood out of their two ears to save from the rack rent and bailiff, or am I going out of my mind?'

I said nothing. I let him at it. I was interested in how he was compressing all the torments I had had over two months inside one hour. He went on and on, half-sobbing like a woman. He puffed away, every now and then finding time to comment on the geographic feature of Mulgannon.

'Oh Lort, the hill, oh Lort!'

I put the cows in the Carraigun field, shut the gate and put a stone to it. I turned on him in a temper to ask where the feckin' hell he'd been for the last four weeks or was it his policy only to appear when disaster struck.

'We'll have to go in and put it up to her, that's what we'll have to do,' I said.

'Put up what?' he snorted. 'Put up my arse. Do you know who you're dealing with, man? That wan is a tartar. Put up is right.'

'We'll have to tell her straight to get shut of your man and we'll have to beat the shit out of him with a horsewhip,' I said.

'You will, ah, you will to be sure have to tell her to get shut of your man, yes, you will, and give him a hiding too, you're a bright spark all right. If you tried to thwart that one inside, if once you tried to cross her, it would all be up. Oh, no, a good job has to be done on this, I'm going to tell you, my boy. But not a word of abuse to her – not a word,' the uncle cautioned.

We got back into the yard and there before us was Moses Flaherty like a motherless foal.

'Dick,' he said, 'this thing is no joke. The lad in the uniform is out for business.'

'Who are you telling?' belched the uncle.

'You haven't heard the latest,' wheezed Mosie Flaherty.

'What?' barked the uncle, crouching sharply around as if expecting an attack.

'He's bought one of the new small cars, a red lad, and he's gone off this minute to Courtown with Kate Furlong in it.'

'Maybe he's gone for the ring,' I said.

'A bull's ring would be more like it,' roared the uncle. 'I'm going. Brains now, men! We'll meet on Monday night in Bob Farrelly's pub in the Swan Square. I want the weekend to think. Not a bloody word now; not a word.'

'I won't open my mouth, anyhow,' declared Moses Flaherty, shuffling his shoulders and rubbing his paws to ease panic.

'Nor I,' I vowed.

We parted. I was not serene in spirit. So great was the fear I had of the unknown that I decided to place the intimate family problem before MacDonagh junior and Mulcahy junior. I later altered my decision, for it didn't take me long to discover that the whole affair was the scoff and jeer of several parishes, and you can throw in the guards' barracks as well. Without me saying a word, a desultory conversation was orchestrated by Mulcahy, supported by MacDonagh, on the appropriate age for marriage and the end for which that sacrament was instituted: namely, the procreation of children.

*

It was only August but the wind swept green leaves over the Swan Square. The rain lashed our faces as Moses Flaherty and I cross-tacked over to Mr Robert Farrelly's licensed premises. Mine host was a large, cheerful man of hospitable demeanour with a well-filled frame and silver hair. He was a man worthy of a second glance, for although busily engaged in the bar and grocery trade, he was a maker and unmaker of government ministers, Dáil Éireann deputies and public representatives. He was also credited with dispensing largesse to party members – the reward of a grateful nation for services to the cause.

The cause which Mr Farrelly served was that of the Fianna Fáil party. This means, in English, the army of the island of destiny. Its head was Mr Éamon de Valera, a man whom neither office nor emolument could buy, a man whose word was his bond, a man who had risen from poverty to become the leader of the Irish race in the universe. My uncle Richard Furlong held that Mr de Valera was the greatest curse that came on the country since Cromwell. The reason for this was that the uncle was of a different political calling.

The uncle was a supporter of the late John Edward Redmond, the leader of the Irish Party in the British House of Commons, a man who shared with Mr de Valera the distinction of being despised and revered by his own people. The party to which Richard Furlong gave allegiance was Fine Gael, which means 'the gathering of the Gael'. There is no difference in appearance or caste between the two parties. The difference is that each occupied opposite positions in the Civil War of 1923 and maintained an antagonism to each other ever since.

The uncle had served the Fine Gael party well. In the parish of Piercestown and Castlebridge, Richard Furlong recruited and organised as devoted a body of supporters as ever reduced a meeting to chaos. He directed struggles to prevent rate and rent collectors' jobs being given to Fianna Fáil party hacks instead of to Fine Gael party hacks. The uncle Dick did not carry the same power on his shoulders as

Mr Farrelly, because Fine Gael had only thirty-eight seats in Dáil Eireann, whereas Fianna Fáil had seventy-six.

Whenever political strife of danger to Fianna Fáil broke out, Mr Farrelly was seen to leave Wexford, attaché case in hand, bound for the trouble area. When problems were resolved he would return, yet he never had his name in the papers and he never sat on any public body or political office. Uncle Dick and he got on together like two rabbits in an orchard. Leaning over the counter in Farrelly's they were all laughs and confidences, as if they used to compare notes on how they wiped opponents' eyes.

When Moses Flaherty and myself entered the public bar, we found Mr Farrelly bent over the counter in his shirt-sleeves, listening with interest to the whispering of Mr Richard Furlong of Poulbrean.

'Two more small Powers, Bob,' ordered the uncle. 'And you're going to drink it too, boy, because you'll want it all before tonight's work is done. Fire a ginger ale into it to take the cut off it.'

'If you've business to discuss, men, you may use the parlour inside.' said Mr Farrelly, 'The stools here have ears.'

We went into the parlour, where a large picture of a nun, a native of Mulgannon, presided.

'Every woman that God ever put the breath of life into has a sore spot,' the uncle said. 'There is one thing that every woman hates. Something that turns her stomach. Are you able to tell me now, boy, what it is that turns that Christian's stomach?' the uncle asked, too bitter to mention the mother by name.

'The mother,' I said, 'has a revulsion against old fecks.'

He turned full around on me.

'What do you mean by "old fecks"?'

'Men who are all gone to religion in public, but follow

and look at women and women's things in private. That's what an old feck is – from the Irish, *feach*, "to look at",' I explained. A brilliant idea sliced through my thoughts.

'I have the very thing,' I announced. 'MacDonagh has a calendar and there's a page for every month in colour and a girl on it in her skin. I could get that sent to her, signed by your man, as a present. He's going away next Friday for a week. She'd never look at the postmark. There'd be some row, I tell you, when he'd get back from Lough Derg.'

The uncle looked at me in disbelief. 'Do you mean MacDonagh, the man who is a bishop in the Knights of Columbanus, a man well over sixty years of age?'

'Not at all,' I snorted. 'His son. The youngest lad. Me and him are pals.'

The uncle swallowed. 'God help Ireland.'

'You'd be wrong, Nick, my poor man,' said Moses Flaherty, 'because a hundred detectives would land on your doorstep, and if you were found out you'd get jail and be preached out from the altar.'

'Have you any brainwaves, you who stand to get the roads of Ireland?' demanded the uncle Richard of the farm horseman.

'I have,' said Flaherty, 'I have several brainwaves and I was awake all last night working them out. The first thing I'd do is shoot the sheepdog and fasten the corpse in the boot of your man's car. Then I'd open it when the woman gets near enough to see.'

I didn't think much of this idea. Apart from the fact that the mother was very attached to the family hound, she was a clever dog after the cows.

'And if that didn't work, I was thinking that a box of well-rotted guts, if they were tied to the bottom of the car and left there to warm up, would be a good idea.'

The uncle was suffering. 'Is it typhoid you had at the back of your mind?'

'Oh, no,' said Flaherty, 'but when the guts begin to bloom near the barracks it will create a hum. Who will he blame but someone in Mulgannon, where the car is always parked? That is, if he's not arrested for spreading disease. He'd have it on his mind that he was being made a hunt of. That would put the skids under him.'

'I wonder was I in my right mind thinking that the two of you were fit to be in my company?' the uncle asked himself. 'Friggin' nonsense and bullshite in a situation like this, with a dangerous lunatic of a woman prepared to hand a place over that was in our hands since before the Rebellion. Or is either of the two of you aware of the way you might be this time twelvemonth? Yah!' he exclaimed with a horrid expression. 'The old man has turned around in the box.'

This reference to the disturbed position of my grandfather's body in Piercestown graveyard had a great effect on us all.

'What will you have, Dick?' asked Mosie Flaherty.

'I will have another half one of course, but give him a tomato juice in case he does anything foolish,' said the uncle.

He was right. I noticed the blood stirring up in me. 'What the hell would you do? You with all the talk,' I made bold to ask him.

His huge girth slumped. He twisted the hard hat on his head. He looked around at me with despairing eyes.

'I'm bet,' he said in a low voice. 'It's a hard thing to face. I'm bet. I've thought of several things. I even thought of heaving him over the quay in the middle of the night. I thought of going up to that woman and seeing to it that you would get the place for certain after her day, but by the time the two of them snuff it, I know God damn well the place would be racked and every shilling scutched to the world. And I'll tell you what you'd be by then, boy. A loon without a tooth in your head.'

The concept of being a pauper as well as a loon without teeth was not pleasurable.

'That's a queer and clever woman. If she once got wind of the word that I was at the back of any conspiracy – goodbye Éireann. I have now come to the conclusion that any move or advice on my part would only drive her on to worse.'

The uncle stifled his emotion with a gurgled whiskey and continued. 'I thought of going up and slapping her on the back and wishing her all the best and "You'll only be young once" – maybe bring up a few of the boys and a case of stout to celebrate. I thought that might alarm her and turn her off the gobshite. But that woman knows me. She'd see me coming a mile away, and nothing I'd do would be worth a damn. Nothing. There is nothing I can do. And if I tried to get your man into trouble, every guard would be on my back. No, I'm bet, boy. The only thing that can save the place now is a first-class miracle, and I'm not on great terms with the Man in charge of that department. Your father has a lot to answer for.'

He did not raise his slumped shoulders but raised his large fist and hammered the table for service. Mr Farrelly entered in discreet quiet.

'We will have three large Powers, Bob, and put a ginger ale in it for the chap. We might as well be killed for a sheep as for a lamb,' the uncle said in tones of hardship.

None of us said anything. What was there to say? Once again I found fear eating me, and even three whiskeys, to which I was ill-accustomed, had done nothing to dull its edge. Gloom – deep gloom – descended on the little party and there was no event or anecdote or song that could blot out the realisation that we were to witness an event which would culminate in the uprooting of a dynasty. I refer to the inevitable marriage of the mother to Guard Benjamin Mary Brodar.

The uncle permitted himself but one other statement, which he addressed to Mosie Flaherty. 'Isn't it desperate to think, after a lifetime of schemes, that I'm unyoked by a woman without her opening her mouth? Drink up, men; we'll go. What the hell would keep us here now?'

We lashed the firewater down and got up to make for the hall door. It was like leaving the wake of a dear old friend. Perhaps this was correct, for had we not placed our hands on the cold forehead of our sacred soil and said there was nothing further we could do?

Out in the hall there was a large framed photograph directly under the light. It showed a very youthful Éamon de Valera with a soft hat, long coat and walking stick, standing on a platform in a wood in County Armagh. He was taking the salute at a march past of the Irish Republican Army around 1921. A long column of marching men with leggings, rifles, cartridge belts and bandoliers were at the 'eyes right' position.

Dick Furlong walked out heavily after me, an aged man. He came by the photograph and looked up at it. The words that trembled on his lips were 'the greatest curse that came on the country since Cromwell'. But that sentence died. He stopped and turned broadside on to the photograph. The frown of hatred deepened as he gazed. Then the frown altered. It altered to a clear visage with no expression at all except the staring eyes. I turned to look at him and I saw. From the great caverns of Heaven, God had planted the mustard seed of an idea in Richard Furlong.

I saw him look at the earnest men, the army of the Gael as they marched in silence by their chief. But to Richard

Furlong there was no silence. I could see it in his face. From that picture there came the first light beat of the battle drum. Then, in the distance, the faint notes of the rebel hymn, 'They rose in dark and evil days to right their native land'.

His bleak eyes took on a twinkle and the racing martial beat grew and grew in his head. Richard Furlong had now two tears on the rough battered face, but he hummed the air, 'De-dum de-dum de-dum de-dum, de-dum de-dum de-dum; They kindled here a living blaze that nothing can withstand.'

A full chorus of men sang back at him from the picture. From the background trees, brass, wind and drums, drums, drums roared to the joy of the hymn he now conducted with his elbows. He sang and laughed and laughed while he raised his conducting arms over his head in joy.

And we laughed and joined in with him while he locked his big arms into ours and winked at me and Mosie Flaherty.

Alas that might can conquer right,
They fell and passed away,
But true men like you men,
Remember still today.

We walked out happy into the teeming rain and gale, drenched, but happy to be alive, for although not another word passed, we knew that a miracle of salvation had been constructed in the brain of Richard Furlong.

*

One week later, the red Mini Minor pulled up with a screech outside our yard gate. There emerged from it a uniformed but hatless Guard Brodar, white in the face. He had the appearance

189

of a man whose braces, pants, combinations, false teeth and scapulars had been wrenched off him and burned before his eyes by his own officers. He shook his head now and again, as if to shift beetles from one side of his skull to the other.

'I'm going, Katherine!' he half-asked. 'I'm going, I've been transferred to Cahirsiveen, three hundred miles away, and I have to report there the day after tomorrow.'

'Blood and ounters,' gasped the mother in Chaucerian English.

I remarked that there was good land as well as a view, and pucks of women there. Well, between the jigs and the reels, he was gone in two days. Gone without a trace or one last wise saying. And do you know what? The mother wasn't a bit put out about him personally, because I asked her. But she smelt a deed by a thwarter which removed Benjamin Mary Brodar. She carried a wicked look around for two weeks, not knowing who or where the enemy was.

The extent of Richard Furlong's devotion and sacrifice was made abundantly clear within a month. It was the time of the Fianna Fáil church-gate annual collection. The mother put one shilling in an envelope and sealed it.

'That's all that's going on the plate, Nicholas,' the mother said. 'Scruff, the lot of them, and they after breaking John Redmond's heart, not to mention the haggards put to the match, but it wouldn't pay to be hostile.'

As the mother and I walked in the main gate of Bride Street churchyard, an awe-inspiring sight thrust its presence upon us. Standing with a collection plate, in his best navy-blue suit, hard hat, shiny white collar and tie, stood my mildly embarrassed uncle, Richard Furlong of Poulbrean. On the lapel of his coat was an election photograph of Éamon de Valera with the legend underneath it, 'For Ireland's sake, vote Fianna Fáil'.

The mother summoned the strength to drop her envelope onto Mr Robert Farrelly's plate. She moved forward until she elevated herself to a better observation point at the priests' graves. Then she wheeled around to focus her eyes on what she had passed. As the aspect of Richard Furlong collecting for the Fianna Fáil party registered in her mind, her jaw fell and a tremble of fury agitated the spare flesh of her chin. I went back and gave him a half-crown with a friendly smile of encouragement.

'A half-crown to those trash! And then the other dolt. I always said that scourge had as many turns as a hare. The sweet, unwholesome louser.'

'It will be time for you to talk, woman,' I said, 'when you've harrowed as much as Dick Furlong has ploughed.'

The mother stopped, clutched her black prayer book and drew up facing him from a distance in order to call down a malediction. To my ears, she declared, 'Plough or no plough, all he ever was, and all he is today, is an old feck.'